T0277806

HOW TO SOUND SMART AT PARTIES

HOW TO SOUND SMART AT PARTIES

An Evening of Fun Facts & Curious Conversations

Michael McBride

Penguin Random House

Publisher Mike Sanders
Executive Editor Alexander Rigby
Editorial Director Ann Barton
Art & Design Director William Thomas
Designer Lindsay Dobbs
Illustrator Pat Corrigan
Copy Editor Devon Fredericksen
Fact Checker Mara Grunbaum
Proofreaders Tamanna Bhasin, Jaye Debber
Indexer Beverlee Day

First American Edition, 2024
Published in the United States by DK Publishing
1745 Broadway, 20th Floor, New York, NY 10019

The authorized representative in the EEA is Dorling Kindersley Verlag
GmbH. Arnulfstr. 124, 80636 Munich, Germany

Library of Congress Number: 2024939244
ISBN 978-0-7440-9094-9

DK books are available at special discounts when purchased
in bulk for sales promotions, premiums, fund-raising, or educational use.
For details, contact SpecialSales@dk.com

Printed and bound in China
www.dk.com

This book was made with Forest
Stewardship Council™ certified
paper – one small step in DK's
commitment to a sustainable future.
Learn more at
www.dk.com/uk/information/sustainability

To my grandfather, who taught me the importance of staying curious until the very end, and to all the tireless teachers who make the world a more curious place.

To whom it may concern:

You are cordially invited to a thrilling and unusual dinner party. I'm bringing together my smartest friends from all over the world . . . and Adam.

There will be cheese.

I cannot guarantee your safety at this party. If your mind is left unattended and allowed to wander, you may find it changed by the time you come back—a risk you'll have to take if you want cheese.

Discussion over dinner is dangerous: the last guest of honor never came back. They said after they learned how strange the world really is, their life was never the same. They also said that the camembert was excellent, easy to spread and with just a hint of nuttiness.

If you'd like to attend, the party will be held just a few pages from now. Try not to get lost on the way there.

If you see something written in bold, it is true to the best of our knowledge. So why discuss it?

Well, "grass is green" is a true statement—except when it is brown.

"The sun rises every day" is a true statement—except in Antarctica and above the Arctic Circle.

If something is written in italics, I'm talking to you directly. Don't worry, the other guests can't hear me—I'm just sharing a secret with you.

Things are rarely as simple as they appear, and neither are the people here. Speaking of which, I should really introduce you!

First, we have **Dick**. Dick is an archaeologist. He spends most of his time covered in sand on various digs in the Middle East. He specializes in ancient civilizations and has an odd penchant for tweed suits.

Dick's girlfriend, **Olivia**, is the complete opposite. She's one of the most popular influencers on the internet. But there's more than meets the eye, as she has published several important papers in the field of linguistics.

Josie is a biologist who spends her time identifying new species of plants and studying gorilla behavior deep in the rainforests of central Africa. She grew up riding horseback, working as a ranch hand in southern Wyoming. No one is tougher than her.

Lloyd is one of the few people I can call a genius without hesitation. NASA has used some of his research, even though he hasn't even fully completed his PhD. The only thing he loves more than rockets is anime.

Izzy is one of America's top psychology researchers. She's a bit of a wild card—a Hungarian immigrant who loves nightlife almost as much as she loves the human mind. Sharp as a tack.

Javier comes from one of the wealthiest families in Colombia—he's taken all that money and put it into research, supporting indigenous studies in the Amazon and elsewhere. No one knows more about South America than him.

Anyway, that's everyone. The smartest people I know . . . and Adam. It should be a fascinating night.

I sincerely hope to see you there.

Yours truly,
M

Adam . . . I think Adam works in sales? I don't know. Super nice guy, though—you'll see.

PS. I have it on good authority that you have an interest in learning how to sound smart at parties. I'll give you some tips throughout the party, but here's the first one: don't try to sound smart. Everyone can see right through it. At first, just listen.

MENU

Hors d'Oeuvres

M: Come on in—the party is just getting started. Can I take your coat? Feel free to take a seat on the couch for some charcuterie with my friends. Let's listen in on them.

When the first Egyptian pyramids were built, woolly mammoths still walked the Earth.

Josie: Most woolly mammoths died out 10,000 years ago, when the last Ice Age ended. But a teeny colony stayed alive on an island off the coast of Siberia.

Dick: They lived there while the first pyramids were built, while the Sumerians wrote the *Epic of Gilgamesh*, and while the ancient Peruvian city of Caral flourished.

Izzy: It makes me sad to think about them. All alone, stuck on that island, as the Earth got warmer and warmer. Wish I could've pet one of them.

M: Izzy loves animals—she'd pet a grizzly bear if it let her. Woolly mammoth fur was a yard (or meter) long!

Bulls don't get angry at the color red. In fact, they can't even see red.

Javier: They actually get angry at the movement of the red cape— that's what makes them charge. The cape is not red for the bull, it's red for the audience.

M: There's a metaphor there somewhere.

Cleopatra's lifetime was closer to the invention of the iPhone than the building of the first pyramid.

Dick: Egypt was already ancient by Cleopatra's time. She lived about 2,000 years ago, but the first pyramid was built around 4,500 years ago.

Lloyd: Wow. What made ancient Egypt last so long?

Dick: The Nile River flooded each year, providing fertile soil for crops. They had a strong cultural identity with a sense of continuity. They survived so many things that ruined other civilizations—the Bronze Age collapse, an endless list of wars, and climate change. But Egypt just kept on with a stiff upper lip!

Adam: I saw a video the other day that said aliens built the pyramids. Supposedly the blocks were too big to be carried by humans.

M: Adam will believe anything. He's wrong, of course—ancient people were much smarter than we think. Modern scientists have recreated how the ancient Egyptians moved the blocks with boats and roller logs.

Apollo astronauts had Velcro patches inside their helmets to scratch their noses.

Lloyd: Itchy noses are a dangerous problem in space. You don't want to sneeze—imagine snot splattering across your helmet while you're trying to navigate the moon!

Izzy: How do astronauts pee?

Lloyd: Funnels and vacuums. They filter the pee to make more drinking water.

Izzy: Gross.

Lloyd: And the poop is loaded into spacecraft and fired at Earth. It burns up in the atmosphere. So the next shooting star you see might be astronaut poop!

M: One small poop for man . . . one giant shooting star for mankind!

The total sewage load in the United States usually peaks at a specific moment every year: Super Bowl halftime.

Lloyd: Sewage systems are actually really hard to design. There's a fundamental paradox: most of the time they stay under capacity, but they have to be built to withstand surges. Like Super Bowl halftime, or even just the daily surge of people showering and getting ready for work.

Adam: I was listening to this podcast the other day about how the avocado industry hired a PR firm to make avocados more popular. They planted the idea (no pun intended) that guacamole and chips were "football-watching foods," perfect for the Super Bowl.

M: This one might sound like a conspiracy, but it's actually true. The California Avocado Growers Exchange also helped change the name from "alligator pear" to "avocado" (for obvious reasons) and hired the PR firm Hill & Knowlton to make it more popular. They held a massive guacamole recipe contest with NFL players during the Super Bowl, leading to an explosion in its popularity.

Former Australian prime minister Bob Hawke once held the world record for chugging a yard glass of beer (that's 2.5 pints) in just 11 seconds.

Dick: Australia has had some strange prime ministers. Harold Holt, for example, just disappeared—he was swept out to sea and his body was never found.

Adam: What do you think happened to him?

Dick: Realistically, he probably drowned after being swept out to sea. But I do hold on to a fantastical hope that it was all an elaborate ruse and he's on a beach somewhere, sipping mojitos, like in a James Bond movie.

M: I wouldn't mind a mojito right now—speaking of which, do you want anything to drink?

When America first banned smoking on airplanes, they made an exception for pilots.

Adam: There's no way that's true!

Olivia: It is. My dad was a pilot, actually. When they first passed the law, people worried that nicotine withdrawals would be dangerous for pilots, so they let them smoke.

Adam: Couldn't they just have chewed some nicotine gum or something?

Josie: You'd think so, wouldn't you? I guess lawmakers didn't think of that!

M: Don't worry—they updated the law and now US pilots can't smoke in the cockpit. But China didn't fully ban pilots from smoking onboard until 2019!

Helium is the only element that was discovered in space before it was found on Earth

Izzy: How's that possible? Surely we had helium before we went to the moon?

Lloyd: This is a crazy story. We can measure what elements are in a star based on the light it emits—you put the light through a spectrometer. In the 1800s, a scientist did this for the sun and saw something he couldn't explain in the spectral signature. There was only one explanation: it must've been a new element. That new element was helium. That's why it's named after Helios, the Greek god of the sun.

Dick: I guess they didn't have helium balloons back then, huh?

Lloyd: Humans didn't really have any usable helium until we started drilling for gas and found it underground. We were like, "What the heck? This is the stuff from the sun."

M: Helium also regularly leaves our planet. When a balloon pops, sometimes that helium floats all the way into space, never to return. If you've ever breathed in helium to make your voice funny, there may eventually be molecules in the outer reaches of our solar system that were once inside your lungs.

There are more ways to shuffle a deck of cards than there are atoms on Earth.

Lloyd: It sounds crazy, but the math is simple. You just multiply 52 × 51 × 50 × 49 . . . all the way down (that's called a "factorial"). The number you end up with is 8 with 67 zeroes, or eighty unvigintillion ways to shuffle the deck. Jeez, I can barely pronounce that! "Unvigintillion" sounds like an anime villain.

But how do we know how many atoms are on Earth? Well, we know the mass of the Earth and we also have a decent idea of the distribution of different elements. With those two numbers, we can estimate the number of atoms.

It turns out, the deck of cards doesn't just win by a little bit. There are six hundred quadrillion times more ways to shuffle a deck of cards than there are atoms on Earth.

Adam: My brain hurts, Lloyd.

M: I'm with Adam on this one.
That's a lot to process!

Drug lord Pablo Escobar owned several hippos. They escaped after his death, and now they are an invasive species in Colombia.

Javier: It's true—they're a real problem for the ecosystem. The government wants to reduce the population, but they're very popular with the people, so they're hesitant to kill them.

Olivia: Did you know that hippos are the most dangerous animal in the world?

M: Well, it depends on your definition. Hippos are the most dangerous "large land mammal." But the humble, miniscule mosquito kills a million people a year. There's a tip for you: if you want to sound smart, anytime someone uses a superlative—most, best, largest, etc.—understand what criteria they're using to make that distinction. Context matters.

The word *sideburns*—to describe facial hair—comes from General Burnside, a Civil War general with impressive muttonchops.

Javier: What a man. *Un hombre real.*

Dick: I think his face looks a bit like a broom.

Izzy: I think he's handsome. Add some tattoos and a bicycle, and you've got my type! I just wanna grab those muttonchops and pull him in for a smooch!

M: My god. I can't take my eyes off those sideburns. They're glorious.

The "toupée fallacy" makes people believe all toupées look bad (because they've never seen a good one).

Izzy: Think about it: if someone had an amazing toupée, you would just think it's their real hair. So, you think every toupée is bad, because every toupée *you've seen* has been bad. If something is designed not to be noticed, then you only notice the bad ones. The same thing applies to plastic surgery.

Adam: Are you trying to tell us that you're wearing a wig right now?

Izzy: You think I'd buy a wig that looks like *this*? I'd sue the store!

M: Izzy just cut her bangs last week. She's worried she looks like Lord Farquaad.

Lead paint wasn't banned in the United States until 1978, and leaded gasoline wasn't completely banned until 1996.

Lloyd: 1996? You're telling me that when the PlayStation was released, gasoline still had lead in it?

Olivia: Sometimes I wonder if everyone just had low-grade lead poisoning back then.

Izzy: Oil companies spent a lot of money trying to convince the public that lead wasn't bad for them. Their main talking point was: "Lead is natural! It comes from the Earth; it can't be bad for you."

Olivia: If that happened today, I think influencers would sell a "lead cleanse."

Izzy: I can see it now: "Patented lead ions attach to toxins and clear your body of impurities! The government HATES lead because they don't WANT us to be healthy! Ancient Romans ate lead—look how muscular they were!"

M: Now don't go giving anyone ideas, Izzy. People might just fall for that!

Some forms of lead taste sweet. Ancient Romans used to flavor their wines with it.

Lloyd: There's even a powdered form of lead called "lead sugar."

Adam: So you're telling me, not only did the Romans have lead in their pipes, they actually put it in their drinks *on purpose*?

Lloyd: It's like they were going for a lead poisoning speed run. Wanna hear something dark? Lead paint sometimes tastes sweet as well. It's one of the reasons lead paint is so dangerous for babies: they eat the paint chips because they're delicious.

Adam: That is dark. I'm not gonna lie, though, I do want to try a little taste.

Olivia: Oh, Adam, what are we gonna do with you?

Paleolithic humans did not necessarily eat a "paleo" diet.

Josie: Up until recently in human history, people ate whatever they could. Every calorie was precious and couldn't be wasted. In some environments—say, the mammoth steppe of the Ice Age—humans had specialized subsistence strategies focused on hunting woolly mammoths and other big game. But we've found plenty of evidence that in other areas, diet was dominated by non-meat sources, even grains.

Adam: Don't tell that to the fitness influencers. They might come for you!

Josie: Don't worry, they won't have the energy after they do Olivia's lead cleanse.

M: Mmm, a lead cleanse and a paleo diet. Just like our ancestors would have wanted!

Appetizers

M: Speaking of drinks, why don't we make our way over to the table for some appetizers and wine. Did you like the cheese? I told you it was good. And the conversation was even better!

For an appetizer tonight, we have candied carrots with feta and stuffed mushrooms. By the way—did you know that vegetables aren't real? "Vegetable" isn't a biological term like "fruit" is. It's just an arbitrary category we have for things we eat. For example, mushrooms are more closely related to humans than they are to carrots, but we still call them "vegetables." Is an herb a vegetable? It's a plant we eat, isn't it? And yet, people would think you were crazy if you called cilantro a vegetable.

Boy, I sure am grateful I don't have the cilantro soap gene. For some people, this delicious herb tastes like soap. Do you have this gene? It's not a problem if you do—I don't think any of the dishes tonight have cilantro.

Come on over to the table, your seat is right there. What do you think of my friends, by the way? They're a strange and charming bunch, aren't they? And my goodness, are they intelligent. Even Adam—though he sometimes doesn't show it. People are smart in different ways and that's okay. Everyone has something to offer. Speaking of which, let's get back to the conversation. The wine should loosen everyone up a bit and make the debate livelier.

There's nothing I love more than a good party with good people!

Romans used to water down their wines, and every party had an "arbiter bibendi" (the "judge of drinking"). He would serve the wine, watering it down if people were partying too hard and making it stronger if things were getting boring.

Javier: It's almost like they had a wine DJ.

Izzy: I think we need one of those here—speaking of which, can someone pour me another glass?

M: Every culture has their own drinking traditions. In Japan, it's considered rude to pour your own sake. In Germany, you must maintain eye contact while toasting or you will supposedly be cursed with seven years of bad sex.

Gravity moves at the speed of light.

Lloyd: Light speed is about much more than just light—which is really trippy to think about. It's the highest possible speed for *any* interaction in nature. It's the universe's speed limit.

Javier: It's also the speed at which Izzy finished her glass of wine. Did you even breathe, Izzy?

Izzy: Hey, it's not often I get to drink wine this nice!

Lloyd: The sun is eight light-minutes away from us. So if it disappeared right now, we'd still have eight minutes of light. But we'd also have eight minutes of the sun's gravity before Earth flew off into space. Which means the sun could have disappeared five minutes ago and we wouldn't even know it.

Javier: How long could we survive without the sun? Would we die instantly?

Lloyd: Well, we'd hardly notice the missing gravity. The sun is so far away it barely affects us, but the missing heat would make things very cold very quickly. Still . . . there is one scenario where we could live. We'd have to get into highly insulated structures underground and use nuclear reactors for heat, or geothermal power like they do in Iceland. If we did this, *theoretically* we could survive for weeks, or even months—maybe even years if we could figure out some way to grow food down there.

Izzy: That makes me feel strangely hopeful, Lloyd. Like humans are going to make it no matter what the universe throws at us.

Lloyd: Don't worry, the sun isn't going to just disappear. Instead, it will slowly expand until it engulfs Earth and explodes.

Javier: I don't think that's any better!

The engineer who built London's sewer system in the 1800s decided to double the size of the pipes. Because of that single decision, those pipes are still in use 150 years later.

Josie: That means that those pipes are older than 14 US states.

Dick: The pipes are older than splinter-free toilet paper.

Josie: Splinter-free? You mean . . .

Dick: Horrifyingly, toilet paper was invented in 1890, but splinter-free toilet paper wasn't invented until 1930.

Josie: You're telling me that for 40 years people just wiped their asses with splinters? Man, I thought the one-ply they use on campus was bad enough.

M: Must have been a rough few decades—literally.

In 1987, American Airlines saved $40,000 by eliminating one olive from every salad served on its planes.

Adam: I learned this in business school. It's an iconic story that shows how every company wants to cut costs.

Izzy: I don't know, I think they may have eliminated too many metaphorical olives. Flying sucks now. What are they going to do next, remove the seats?

M: Fewer olives also meant less weight and therefore less fuel. They also saved weight by not painting the planes—paint is heavier than you'd think!

Humans can survive several minutes in outer space without a space suit.

Adam: Wait, wouldn't our blood boil? Wouldn't we explode or freeze solid?

Lloyd: Not exactly. Liquids boil in outer space because there is no air pressure to hold the molecules together. But your blood is different. Your blood is in a closed system—your circulatory system. Your veins and arteries would maintain enough pressure to stop it from boiling. We also wouldn't freeze, for a reason that feels very counterintuitive.

Adam: What? But isn't outer space, like, ridiculously cold?

Lloyd: Yes and no. There's not much heat there, but there also isn't very much matter to conduct heat away from us. Think about it this way: when you are wet, you lose warmth faster, right?

Adam: Yeah.

Lloyd: Think about the reverse of that. The extreme reverse. There's almost nothing in space—no water, no air—nothing to touch our skin and take the warmth away. So although the temperature itself is low, we lose heat very slowly. It would take hours to fully freeze. What kills us in space is much simpler: the vacuum forcefully sucks all the air out of our lungs. You die within a few minutes from good old suffocation. And cruelly, gas in our intestines is also forced out from the other end.

Adam: So you're telling me you'd die in space with a monster fart? That's rough.

M: Maybe it could propel you back to your spacecraft!

George Washington may be shirtless on many US quarters.

Adam: It's been hiding in plain sight this whole time. Who has a quarter here? It has to be made before 2022. Let's look at it. You can see Washington's *clavicle*. That man is not wearing a shirt. It's clear as day. The artist who designed it also had a penchant for shirtless, Greek-style portraits of important men.

Olivia: Reminds me of that statue of Washington that used to be in the White House. He was in a toga, with wildly unnecessary six-pack abs. So bizarre. Look at this photo if you don't believe me!

Javier: Wow. He looks like Ryan Gosling in this. And this was in the White House?

Olivia: For a bit. They removed it out of embarrassment!

In English, adjectives almost always follow a very specific order.

Olivia: You already know this, but you don't know that you know it. You say, "a great big pink pig" because "a pink big great pig" just sounds wrong.

Generally, we say adjectives in this specific order:

1	2	3	4	5	6	7	8
Quantity or number	Quality or opinion	Size	Age	Shape	Color	Proper adjective	Purpose or qualifier
two	great	big	old	round	pink	American	pigs

So you'd have: two great big old round pink American pigs.

Any different sounds bizarre: you can't have "American old big great two pink round pigs." It makes your brain short-circuit just hearing it.

Dick: Reminds me of ablaut reduplication!

Adam: What's ablaut reduplication?

Ablaut reduplication is when, if a word is repeated twice with a changed vowel, the first word almost always has an *i* and the second word an *a* or *o*.

M: *I know it's confusing. It makes more sense when you see examples.*

Dick: It's *ticktock*, not *tocktick*. *Chitchat*, not *chatchit*. There are too many examples to count: knickknack, clip-clop, hip-hop, kitty cat, ping-pong, splish-splash. Try to see if you can think of any counterexamples—there really aren't any.

Javier: English has so many unwritten rules, *dios mío*! How do you expect anyone to learn all of these?

Izzy: Don't worry, Javier. Your English is perfect.

The English language is more closely related to Hindi than Chinese is to Japanese.

Olivia: This is an incredible fact. One of my favorites. There was this ancient language (that we now call Proto-Indo-European) that spread a ridiculous distance all over the world. It is the ancestor of languages as diverse as Spanish, English, Portuguese, Hindi, Urdu, Bengali, Russian, Punjabi, German, Persian (Farsi), French, Marathi, Italian, and Gujarati. I'm out of breath just naming them!

Adam: What a wild mix of languages.

Olivia: By contrast, Chinese and Japanese are almost totally unrelated. It's a bit confusing because Japan adapted China's writing system in the fifth century CE, so the written languages look kind of similar.

King Charles VIII of France died after hitting his head on a doorway.

Dick: He joins the illustrious ranks of monarchs who died hilariously tragic deaths: Henry I of England died after eating too much fish. Louis II of Hungary died after falling into a small stream (he couldn't stand up because his armor was too heavy). Edmund II of England may have been stabbed by an assassin who hid in his toilet.

Adam: Probably scared the crap out of him!

M: I should note that there are conflicting sources on how Edmund II died. I hope, for his sake, it wasn't on the toilet.

The biomass of ants is greater than the combined biomass of ALL wild birds and mammals.

Josie: It gets even crazier in rainforests. They can make up 25 percent of the animal biomass in a rainforest—a quarter of all animals there. Everything is just covered in ants, sometimes the ground looks like it's moving.

Izzy: I had a crappy apartment that was like that once. I don't miss being that broke!

Josie: I've had more ant bites in the field than I can count. But gosh, I do find ants fascinating. In the rainforest, leafcutter ants don't even eat the leaves. They take cuttings back to their nests and use them to grow fungus. Then, they eat THAT FUNGUS. Which means ants literally have their own kind of "agriculture."

M: For this purpose, leafcutter ants slice up one-fifth of all new plant growth in the Amazon!

Colonies of army ants can form "raids" the length of football fields. These raids consist of millions of ants.

Josie: I've seen it before, y'all, while doing field research in Africa. They're terrifying. They march along the forest, eating everything in sight. A colony can consume half a million animals every day. They even eat small vertebrates, like baby birds and turtles.

Instead of nests, army ants make bivouacs out of their own bodies, transforming into massive balls of ants to protect themselves. Truly a nightmare.

M: Anyone else feel itchy all of a sudden?

"Buffalo buffalo buffalo Buffalo buffalo Buffalo buffalo buffalo" is a valid English sentence.

Olivia: Buffalo can mean multiple things: the animal, the city in New York, and a verb that roughly means "to bully." So this bizarre sentence means: "Buffalo from the city of Buffalo, New York, bully other buffalo from Buffalo, New York—who in turn are bullied by a third group of buffalo who also happen to hail from Buffalo, New York."

Javier: I really think the person who invented English was a sadist.

Olivia: You could even double the sentence size and it's still a valid English sentence—there would just be more groups of buffalo.

M: Theoretically, you could extend this sentence infinitely and it would still basically work.

An acre of peanuts can make 30,000 peanut butter sandwiches.

Lloyd: That's why George Washington Carver was the GOAT.

Adam: Greatest of all time? The peanut butter guy?

Lloyd: That's actually a myth—he didn't invent peanut butter. He did something way more important. The South was absolutely ravaged after the US Civil War, and the legacy of slavery was in the soil. Cotton depletes the soil it's grown in, so large portions of land were borderline unusable. Carver promoted crop rotation and the planting of legumes like peanuts, which put nitrogen back into the soil and provided nutritious food for the population. He helped save the economy of the South and improved the lives of small-scale farmers.

M: Carver promoted hundreds of uses for peanuts, including—you guessed it—peanut butter.

If you put a mouse wheel in the middle of a field, wild mice will run on it.

Josie: I always assumed mice were just bored in their cages, but I guess they love running on wheels? I wonder why, evolutionarily. I suppose humans get endorphins from running, so maybe mice do, too? Mice that love running probably survive a lot longer than those that hate it. That might be just enough evolutionary pressure to encourage that trait. A "runner's high" for mice, if you will.

Javier: Can you imagine the thought process of the mice that didn't make it? "Oh, I hate running so much, I think I'll just let this hawk eat me."

Josie: Honestly, I feel like that some days during marathon training.

M: Don't forget that applying this type of logic to evolution is "post hoc" analysis. Figuring out why traits persisted in a species is often speculative without hard data.

Ninety-nine percent of a fart doesn't smell. The 1 percent that does is mostly hydrogen sulfide (and smells very bad).

Dick: I think for Olivia it's probably closer to 5 percent. They really are deadly, honey.

Olivia: Dick! I guess you're sleeping on the couch tonight, then.

Dick: Oh, come on, it was just a joke!

M: Take note here: sometimes being smart isn't just knowing what to say, it's knowing when to shut up!

In 1919, just after World War I ended, only 6 percent of homes in the UK had access to electricity.

Dick: We forget how recently the world was electrified. World War I was mostly lit by kerosene.

Adam: Kerosene is also how Rockefeller first got rich. Everyone thinks it was because of gasoline, but the first big oil boom was due to the demand for kerosene. Before that, most lamps used whale oil.

M: Whale oil was a major reason whaling was such a profitable profession. As a matter of fact, for a brief period, the whaling town of New Bedford, Massachusetts, was the wealthiest city per capita in America.

Penicillin was once so valuable they filtered the urine of patients who'd taken it to recycle and extract more.

Josie: When penicillin was invented, it was exceedingly hard to manufacture because the drug requires a finicky, slow-growing mold. So penicillin's British inventors went to the United States to try to find companies that could produce industrial quantities of the antibiotic for the planned Allied invasion of Europe in World War II.

Dick: I guess they needed P-Day before D-Day, huh?

Josie: Nice dad joke, Dick. Scientists searched all over for faster-growing strains of this mold—they finally found one on a random cantaloupe in a fruit market in Peoria, Illinois. A small Brooklyn company helped them manufacture large batches. That company's name? Pfizer.

Adam: Are they paying you to say that?

Josie: It's literally just history, Adam. Not everything is a conspiracy.

M: Why did the two melons plan a big wedding? Because they cantaloupe.

The first electric sidewalk was invented in 1893, debuting at the World's Fair.

Josie: That's why technological progress is so weird: if you had seen an electric sidewalk in 1893 and rode it in a giant loop down the pier, you'd have thought it was a technological miracle and the whole world would soon be covered with moving sidewalks. Instead, we only have them in airports, and half the time they're turned off.

Izzy: There's actually some interesting psychology around moving sidewalks. People walk slower on them, so they only minimally improve travel times. That's one reason they never really caught on. People compensate and ruin all the benefits. Human psychology is weird.

M: We invented the electric sidewalk before we invented tea bags!

The average American watches four hours of television per day.

Izzy: Just numbing themselves to the existential dread of modern existence, you think?

Adam: Or enjoying the beautiful bounty of the golden age of television?

Javier: *Dios mío.* You can get a lot done in four hours.

Adam: I wonder if the median is any different than the average? Like, is the upper end of television watching so extreme it pulls the numbers up? Or is the bottom end of folks who don't watch at all pulling it down?

M: Adam's learning! Differentiating between average and median statistics is a surefire way to sound smart at parties and avoid misinformation.

Paleontologists sometimes lick rocks to find out if they are fossils. If the stone sticks to your tongue, it's a fossil.

Josie: That's because fossilized bone is more porous than rock. There are also certain salty minerals you can taste.

Adam: I wonder how dinosaur bones taste!

M: Don't try this at home.

Modern dry cleaning was discovered by accident after someone spilled kerosene on their tablecloth and it became cleaner.

Lloyd: Dry cleaning isn't dry—it just uses chemical solvents instead of water. In the 1800s they used kerosene and other flammable solvents. Predictably, many of these places exploded or caught fire. Fortunately, we use different chemicals today.

M: A dry cleaner that used kerosene? That's what I call a "no smoking" workplace!

If you brought just a tablespoon of a neutron star to Earth, it would weigh 10 billion tons. At that density, you could fit all humans on Earth into a standard six-sided dice.

Lloyd: Neutron stars are the collapsed core of a massive supergiant star. They are the densest thing we know of other than black holes.

Javier: Will our sun turn into a neutron star?

Lloyd: No, it's not big enough. It will eventually end its life as a sad, glowing, white dwarf star. But not before turning into a red giant and consuming Mercury and Venus (and possibly Earth). But don't worry, we still have five billion years.

Adam: You're saying the sun's small? I don't know, looks pretty big to me.

M: Gosh, Lloyd really talks a lot about the sun consuming us. Maybe I should give him a call after this and make sure he's doing okay!

The "IKEA Effect" is a cognitive bias where we attach higher value to something we build ourselves.

Izzy: Humans are inherently irrational. "Cognitive biases" are what we call predictable patterns of deviation from rationality in judgment.

Adam: What are some others?

Izzy: How about anchoring bias? It's the reason stores often put their most expensive items at the entrance. If there's a $500 sweater sitting on the table, a $30 shirt seems cheap. Our brains get "anchored" to the higher price point. Hell, the store might not even be trying to sell $500 sweaters—they might just be there to make the shirts seem cheaper!

M: There's also confirmation bias, which you need to be very careful of. That's our bias toward only seeking information which confirms our preexisting beliefs. We're especially vulnerable to this while fact-checking.

Humans hadn't photographed a living giant squid until 2004.

Josie: That's because giant squids usually live deep in the ocean. They're massive. The largest giant squid we've seen is 43 feet (13 meters) long. That's as big as a four-story building!

Lloyd: I wonder what else in the ocean we haven't discovered?

M: As mysterious and wonderful as this is, it ignores the fact that we've found dead giant squids since at least 1861—so we very much knew of their existence. Always be wary of how facts are worded. Giant squids are also possibly the inspiration for many mythical creatures, like the Kraken and the Loch Ness Monster!

The Antarctic blue whale is likely the largest animal that has ever existed. It can weigh up to 400,000 pounds (181 metric tons).

Josie: We haven't found any dinosaurs that are larger than the modern blue whale. As a matter of fact, some scientists theorize that blue whales are approaching the upper limit of how big an animal can *possibly* be, due to certain properties of physics and biology. To move its blood around, a blue whale needs to have a heart the size of a small car. To survive, it needs to eat over 8,000 pounds (3,629 kilograms) of krill per day!

More people have been to the moon than to the deepest part of the ocean.

Lloyd: Well, they're both pretty hard to get to. The deepest part of the ocean is called the "hadal zone." It's almost completely dark and the pressure can be ONE THOUSAND TIMES stronger than what we experience sitting here. That's just impossible to fathom.

Olivia: No pun intended.

M: *Get it, fathom? Like the nautical measurement?*

Main Course

M: I'd krill for some dinner right now—I'm ready to eat 8,000 pounds of the main course! I hope you're still hungry after eating all those stuffed mushrooms! We'll be having a gorgeous roast lamb and—are you vegan or vegetarian? We have some amazing fried eggplant if you are.

Did you know that, botanically speaking, eggplants are a type of berry? But strawberries and raspberries aren't.

That is one of the things I love most about science. As we peel back the layers of our world, we consistently uncover little morsels of delight that challenge expectations about the way things "should" be.

The universe does not owe us consistency. It has no duty to make sense. And thank goodness, because life would be phenomenally boring were that not the case.

For sides, we'll be having potatoes au gratin, candied Brussels sprouts, and a Mediterranean garbanzo bean salad that is to die for.

Bon appétit!

The Amazon River accounts for 15 percent of all fresh water dumped into the ocean by all rivers in the world. There is an island in the mouth of the Amazon River about the size of Switzerland.

Javier: The Amazon River is massive. I've spent a lot of time exploring it while working on research projects. During the wet season, it rises over 30 feet (9 meters), flooding the surrounding forests. It can be wider than 30 miles (48 kilometers) in places. Thirty miles!

Dick: That's almost as wide as this rack of lamb. My goodness, I've never seen a roast like this! It's delicious!

M: In parts of the Amazon, they need two maps—one for the wet season and one for the dry season—because the landscape changes so dramatically.

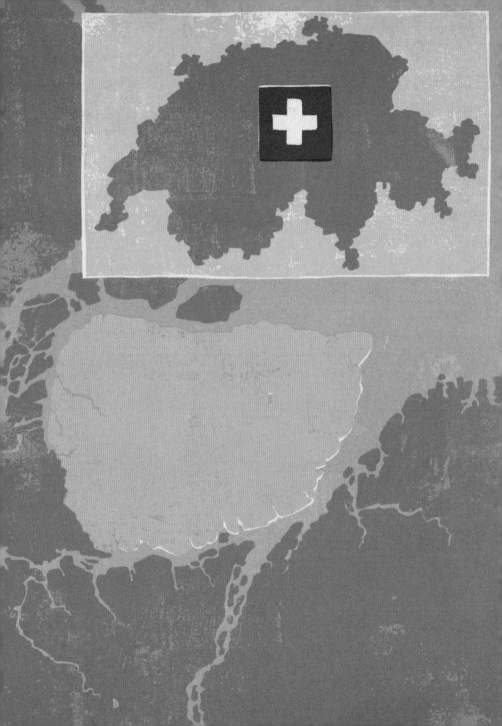

Ninety percent of the Mesopotamian tablets we've discovered have never been translated or even examined in detail by an expert.

Adam: There's no way that's true.

Dick: It is. Trust me, I've spent most of my life in the field! For most eras, we have too little writing; but for ancient Mesopotamia, we have the opposite problem. We have tablets from accountants, politicians, letters from children to their parents, and even the first recorded customer complaint in history: the famous copper complaint to Ea-nāsir.

Adam: Can't we use AI to translate them?

Dick: There are actually a few projects working on that right now that I'm optimistic about!

M: Imagine getting a business review so bad people are still reading it 4,000 years later.

We mostly breathe out of one nostril at a time.

Josie: We've got this weird thing with our noses: there's erectile tissue there that makes one nostril do about 75 percent of the work. It switches every few hours, in cycles of congestion and decongestion. We're not sure why this happens evolutionarily, but some have speculated that it's to ensure one nostril always stays moist.

M: Why am I breathing on manual all of a sudden?

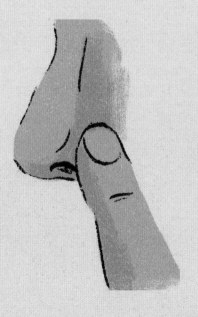

The Inca Empire is the largest continuous north-to-south empire that has ever existed.

Dick: Most empires and trade routes in history were west-to-east or east-to-west, like the Silk Road. Think about it: at the same latitude there is less variation in climate. North-to-south is much harder. The Inca Empire included one of the driest deserts in the world, some of the highest snowy mountains, and parts of the Amazon rainforest. Ten million people lived under Inca rule at the empire's height, in wildly varied climates and landscapes.

Javier: The Inca were a proper empire, as significant as the Greeks or the Romans or the Persians, in my eyes. Many of the roads, aqueducts, and buildings they built are still in use today. As a matter of fact, most of the modern city of Cusco was built on Inca foundations. They even had their own system of writing, which involved the use of a series of knots.

M: You have to be careful—writing can mean many different things. The "quipu" knots may have served as more of a memory aid than a full-fledged system of writing. But there's no way to know for sure—the Spanish colonizers burned most of the quipus.

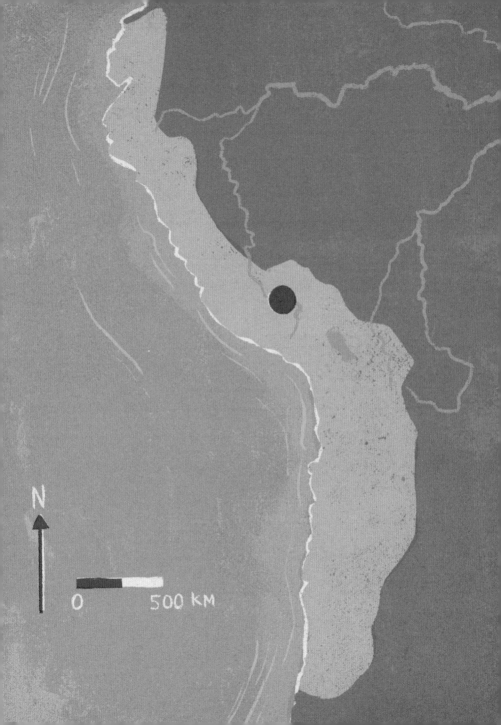

In a group of 23 people, there is a 50 percent chance that two of them have the same birthday.

Adam: How is that possible?

Lloyd: It's called the "birthday paradox." It's hard to explain the math, but think about it this way: although there are only 23 people, there are 253 total *pairs* of birthdays, because for each person, there are 22 potential pairs. With 253 chances, the odds that *none of them* are the same are quite low. If you really want to nerd out, here's the formula:

$$\left(\frac{364}{365}\right)^{253} = .4995$$

The odds of any single pair of birthdays *not* being the same is 364/365. That to the power of 253 (for 253 pairs) gives you the odds of *no* birthdays being the same—49.95 percent, making the odds of a matching pair 50.05 percent.

Adam: Makes total sense! Is there any more cheese for the potatoes?

M: If someone is throwing numbers at you, it's okay to ask them to slow down and explain it to you. Otherwise, you will end up like Adam here, who doesn't get it and is just pretending.

Lloyd: Don't think about 23 people. Just imagine the odds of 253 random pairs of birthdays, and everything becomes a lot more intuitive.

Adam: Okay, I actually get it now.

M: There we go, that's much better. Truly smart people can almost always explain complex concepts simply. To me, it's the mark of a great mind.

Christopher Columbus was arrested for mishandling his governmental position in the Caribbean, based on reports of extreme brutality inflicted on the indigenous islanders.

Javier: Columbus was a *particularly* bad man. Not just by our standards today, but even back then. And let me tell you: the Spanish Empire did not set a high bar for morality, so if they thought you were pushing it, you were really some kind of psychopath.

Dick: They arrested him, didn't they?

Javier: They did. Do you know how cruel of a colonist you had to be to get arrested by the Spanish Empire? *Dios mío!*

Wombats poop cubes. Scientists aren't sure why.

Josie: The best theory right now is that it has something to do with wombats marking their territory—cubes don't roll away when deposited on rocks and logs. But other scientists say it's just due to the dry environments they live in; their intestines squeeze out all the water from food and make the poop cube-shaped.

Olivia: Wombats are so cute, they can poop in whatever shape they want.

M: Maybe wombats have just been playing too much Minecraft!

White sand is mostly parrotfish poop.

Josie: Parrotfish scrape algae off rocks and coral, then they poop out the bits of coral they can't digest. Those undigested bits are what soft white sand is made of. Think about that next time you're lying on a beach in Hawaii.

Olivia: I want to build a time machine so I can go back to before I learned this fact.

M: Olivia loves to vacation in Hawaii. Maybe not anymore!

Around 10 percent of the country of Tuvalu's GDP comes from lending out the ".tv" domain.

Izzy: They really won the lottery on that one, huh?

Olivia: And the ".io" domain is owned by the British Indian Ocean Territory. They make money renting it out, too. Some random small countries really lucked out by having names that corresponded with abbreviations for sought-after domains.

Izzy: The weirdest domain is ".su"—that was the domain for the Soviet Union!

Olivia: Isn't it crazy to think the internet and the Soviet Union existed at the same time? I think of them both as two very different eras.

M: The Soviet Union fell 15 months after it was assigned its ".su" domain.

Some people (especially children) can regrow their fingertips if they are cut off.

Josie: This is really weird. It only happens if the finger is cut above the base of the nail. Scientists think there's a type of cell at the base of our nails that helps it regrow.

M: We're unsure why sometimes fingertips regrow and sometimes they don't. Age appears to be a big factor, as well as how much of the fingertip was cut off.

The nails on your dominant hand grow faster, so do the nails on longer fingers.

Josie: It's mostly a blood flow thing. Your dominant hand is moving more, hitting into things. And those small traumas cause growth. Longer fingers have more blood flow and hit into more things, too. Although, jeez, you'd think with how banged up my hands get working on the ranch my nails would grow like lightning!

Adam: I always thought my thumbnails grew more slowly . . .

M: Scientists still aren't 100 percent sure why this happens or to what extent.

The Great Library of Alexandria didn't disappear in one big fire. It likely deteriorated due to neglect.

Dick: There are a lot of misconceptions about the Great Library of Alexandria—first off, most of the books there were actually copies. The king sent for books from all over the world, made copies, then returned the books.

Izzy: Like an ancient version of BitTorrent, just all copies.

Dick: A little bit. Contrary to popular belief, there wasn't some massive inferno that destroyed all the world's knowledge at once. There were a few fires, sure, but the library recovered. However, it couldn't survive neglect. A lack of resources and interest meant that the library slowly faded away, disappearing as a center of knowledge and learning.

M: Jeez, talk about a metaphor. Not with a bang, but a whimper.

Pearl Harbor could have been much worse if not for a Japanese miscommunication.

Adam: This is a weird one. When Japanese fighter pilots were coming in, they had a signal system: one flare if the attack was a surprise, two flares if they had been spotted. The squadron leader shot one flare into the air, because it *was* a surprise. But he thought that one of his pilots hadn't seen it, so he fired a second flare. Now, everyone else obviously thought this was the two-flare signal—how could they not? And so they started shooting too early, which may have made it less dangerous for the US Navy ships in the harbor. The Japanese pilots were supposed to wait for the slower torpedo planes, which would have sunk even more ships.

M: Their bad luck, America's good luck, I suppose.

The brand Nike gets its name from the Greek goddess of victory.

Olivia: And Adidas was named after its founder, Adolf "Adi" Dassler.

Adam: What about Puma?

Olivia: That's just named after the animal. But weirdly enough, it was founded by Adi Dassler's brother. Talk about a power family.

Izzy: I saw in a video that the founders of Aldi and Trader Joe's are also brothers!

Adam: What about Reebok?

Olivia: There's an African antelope called a "rhebok."

Adam: What about Air Jordan?

Olivia: You're kidding, right?

M: The Air Jordan is, of course, named after basketball legend Michael Jordan.

At age 23, Ernest Hemingway lost almost everything he had ever written, including an unfinished novel.

Olivia: His wife traveled to meet him and brought all his writings in a suitcase. That suitcase was stolen. When she told her husband what had happened, she couldn't stop crying. Hemingway laughed and told her not to worry because he had carbon copies of all his writing back home. The problem was: she had taken the copies, too. His writing was gone forever.

Dick: After everything was gone, Hemingway started over. The first thing he wrote?: *The Sun Also Rises*, his first commercially successful book. He'd later say he was glad the first novel disappeared, because it wasn't any good.

Izzy: Same thing happened to the band Green Day—the master tapes of an entire album were stolen before its release. They decided to start over completely and the next album they made was the uber-successful *American Idiot*.

M: There are just two things you need to be careful not to lose: your mind and your temper.

Author Hunter S. Thompson was purportedly such a severe alcoholic he had to be given IV alcohol during surgery to avoid withdrawal symptoms.

Adam: You know, that's a pretty sad way to live, but at least you know he wasn't lying about his persona.

M: "Fear and loathing," indeed.

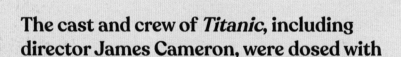

The cast and crew of *Titanic*, including director James Cameron, were dosed with PCP, a highly hallucinogenic substance.

Adam: This is the wildest story ever. Someone—maybe a vengeful caterer, but to this day, no one knows for sure—decided to put PCP in the clam chowder. And so, everyone who ate the chowder started hallucinating. People had to go to the hospital. James Cameron got stabbed in the face with a pen by a crew member.

Javier: "I'm the king of the world!"

M: Although this fact sounds like an insane conspiracy theory, it's actually been corroborated by multiple witnesses. As far as we know, Leonardo DiCaprio managed to avoid the chowder.

The "pompadour" hairstyle comes from a woman named Madame de Pompadour.

Olivia: That's not even a pompadour! It's just an updo!

Izzy: Yeah, I'm curious how we went from that to greasers riding motorcycles in the 1950s. Language is weird.

Lloyd: Did you know there's an entire greaser/rockabilly subculture in modern Japan? They dress like greasers from the '50s, with big, slicked-back pompadours and leather jackets.

M: Honestly, they seem like they're having a great time.

In 1795, French *cavalry* captured a fleet of *ships*—one of the only times in history men on horseback captured boats.

Dick: This seems impossible, right? Did the horses swim?

Adam: The Dutch had miscalculated the weather, and ice surrounded a fleet of their ships. The French tied fabric around their horses' hooves and rode out on the ice to capture the ships.

Javier: This only happened one other time—during the war for Venezuela's *independencia*. José Antonio Páez and 50 brave men swam on horseback through a river full of alligators. They captured 14 boats—and surprised the hell out of the Spanish sailors!

M: Probably surprised the horses, too!

We still use medical leeches.

Dick: I guess those crazy medieval doctors weren't totally wrong!

Josie: They're only used in very specific circumstances. For example, they can sometimes improve blood flow following a tissue reattachment procedure.

Dick: It's funny to think that *barbers* used to administer leeches. Can you imagine? My barber can barely cut my hair these days, let alone bleed me out. Some real Sweeney Todd vibes back then, huh?

M: Leeches are used to stop blood from coagulating in a medical setting. This occasionally saves limbs!

For over 30 years, plastic Garfield the cat telephones have washed up on French beaches.

Olivia: A shipping container full of Garfield phones fell off a ship near the coast, and they've been washing up ever since.

Izzy: I just listened to a podcast on this—it was a mystery for decades until recently, when they found an underwater cave full of Garfield telephones.

Olivia: Imagine how confused some French fisherman must have been when he found the first couple of them!

M: "Monsieur, qu'est-ce que Garfield?"

The US Army's School of the Americas trained 11 future Latin American dictators.

Izzy: Ah yes, that lovely "anti-communism" military school produced such wonderful alumni as Manuel Antonio Noriega and several founders of the Mexican cartel "Los Zetas."

Javier: Overthrowing Latin American governments is like a hobby for the United States, no?

Izzy: They literally had classes on how to torture more effectively— from lessons we learned in Vietnam, apparently.

M: These issues are usually more complex than they seem at face value—America tried very hard to fight "communism" in Latin America, and it had some serious unintended consequences. Many countries were destabilized or left with a strongman in charge.

In Georgian, *shemomechama* means: "the feeling when you are full but keep eating anyway because it tastes good."

Josie: That's a word I didn't know I needed. Speaking of which, can someone pass the lamb?

M: Are you enjoying your dinner? Personally, I'm currently feeling very shemomechama.

The word *kamikaze* means "divine wind," and originally referred to the typhoons that saved Japan from two separate Mongol invasions.

Dick: The Mongols were never able to take over Japan because their fleet was destroyed by storms not once, but *twice*. Seventy thousand Mongol men were captured. After the second time, the Mongols were just like, "Screw it, we're not going back there."

M: As crazy as it sounds, from what we know of history, this seems to be true.

World War II rationing created clothing trends that still influence how we dress today.

Dick: Fabric was rationed—because, of course, the troops needed uniforms. So clothing that needed extra fabric—like double-breasted jackets, or pleated pants—fell out of fashion.

Olivia: There were also rations on stockings because they used nylon to make parachutes!

In Renaissance-era Europe, sugar was so prized that kings and queens displayed sugar sculptures called "subtleties."

Dick: Well, think about it: if you go way back, they didn't really have sugarcane in Europe. If you wanted something sweet, honey was the main option. Soldiers coming back from the Crusades brought sugar from the Arab world and called it "sweet salt." Originally, they thought of sugar more as medicine than food.

Josie: It wasn't until sugarcane was cultivated using slave labor in Caribbean colonies that the price of sugar started to drop.

M: I feel like a giant sugar sculpture isn't very "subtle."

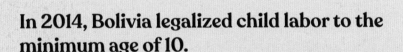

In 2014, Bolivia legalized child labor to the minimum age of 10.

Dick: Now, this might sound cruel, but they had their reasons. Supposedly, there is so much child labor in Bolivia that they legalized it to protect child workers and help them get minimum wage. It's the same argument behind legalizing prostitution or gambling—better to have it in the open where you can regulate it.

Olivia: I'm skeptical about whether this improved things or not.

M: Bolivia's policies were extremely controversial, and experts have mixed opinions on whether they've been effective in protecting child workers. In 2018, Bolivia revised the minimum age to 14.

In World War I, Germany rationed sausages because they needed cow intestines to make zeppelins.

Adam: Yes, those giant balloons in the sky were made almost entirely from intestines.

Javier: It's funny, it's easy to forget there weren't many plastics back then. They had to be creative.

M: I can't imagine how controversial sausage restrictions were in Germany, of all places.

During "Exercise Tiger," a practice drill for D-Day, Allied ships fired live rounds. Up to 450 Americans were accidentally killed.

Adam: Eisenhower insisted on simulating real battle conditions using live rounds to harden the men for D-Day and the Allied invasion of Europe. It ended poorly when there was a huge friendly fire incident.

M: That isn't even the craziest part of the story. The next day, German boats attacked the exercises, which almost gave away plans for D-Day!

World War I made beards unpopular because soldiers had to be clean-shaven to ensure their gas masks had a tight seal.

Adam: Look at pictures of American presidents. Many have facial hair . . . until 1913. During World War I, beards became associated with people who didn't serve in the military.

Dick: It's also why Adolf Hitler had that distinctive mustache. He shaved the sides off so that his gas mask would fit.

Adam: Soldiers needed to shave regularly, and so King C. Gillette manufactured 32 million disposable razor blades—a new invention at the time.

M: After the war, they let soldiers keep their razors, and King C. Gillette made a fortune selling razor blades. You probably recognize his last name from store shelves today. By the way—King was just his name. He wasn't royalty or anything. He was from Wisconsin.

It's almost impossible to ignite gasoline with a cigarette. Researchers tried 4,500 times and failed.

Lloyd: You know in movies when someone throws a cigarette behind them into a puddle of gasoline, and they walk away all badass as it explodes? Well, that's unbelievably unlikely. The temperature at which a cigarette burns is usually not hot enough.

Adam: Then why do gas stations have "No Smoking" signs?

Lloyd: Because people *light* cigarettes. And the flame from a lighter is certainly hot enough to cause gasoline to ignite.

M: Reminds me of that famous scene in Zoolander—*the "freak gasoline fight accident."*

Hawaii was once home to a "leper colony" of over 1,000 people.

Olivia: There's an isolated part of an island where they forced people with leprosy to live for, like, over 100 years.

Josie: Leprosy is contagious and it can disfigure people, so lots of societies throughout history have treated it with fear. Turns out it's completely curable with antibiotics.

Olivia: They turned the island into a National Historical Park, but there are actually still a handful of former leprosy patients who live there.

M: Hawaii's leprosy isolation law wasn't lifted until 1969. Ironically, leprosy doesn't even spread that easily, as 95 percent of all people are naturally immune to the disease.

There is a small chance that the first object the United States sent into space may have been a nuclear "manhole cover."

Lloyd: So, this is wild—the United States was conducting nuclear tests in 1954 and decided to do a test inside of a mountain. They dug a giant hole, then covered it with a piece of metal and set off an atomic bomb inside. Predictably, the top was blown off, but it was blown off with a velocity that may have been six times the escape velocity of Earth. Theoretically, under perfect conditions, it could have gone into space. But realistically, it is far more likely that it vaporized in the atmosphere.

M: An analyst involved in the project believes the metal cover likely burned up, but I love to think there might be a lone manhole cover floating somewhere in space!

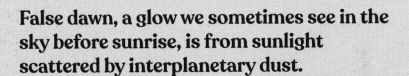

False dawn, a glow we sometimes see in the sky before sunrise, is from sunlight scattered by interplanetary dust.

Javier: We call the very early morning *madrugada* in Spanish. You don't have a word for that time in English, do you?

Lloyd: Well, no—I just call it "time to go back to sleep." But the blue glow in the sky is "false dawn."

M: It's poetic, isn't it? The dust reflecting the sun? Even dirt, under the right circumstances, reflects beauty.

During World War II, a hospital in Italy created a fictitious illness to scare Nazi officials away and save the lives of Jewish patients.

Olivia: They called it "Syndrome K"—a new disease the Italian doctors had identified (invented), which was highly contagious and deadly. Any time a Nazi soldier was around, doctors told the Jewish "patients" to cough as loudly as they could. The soldiers didn't want to catch this horrible new disease, so they stayed away.

Dick: Pretty smart, especially considering they were putting their own lives at risk if anyone discovered they were lying.

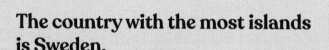

The country with the most islands is Sweden.

Olivia: Sweden? That's wild. I would have thought it was Indonesia or the Philippines or something. What does Sweden even look like? Can someone pull up a map on their phone?

Dick: Ah, I see. It's a lot of very small islands on the coast. No wonder the Vikings became great sailors.

M: Sweden has more than 267,000 islands, and only 1,000 of them are occupied! Norway is a close second, with 239,000 islands.

Alcatraz, the famous high-security prison off the coast of San Francisco, was one of the only prisons at the time to offer hot showers to its inmates. Guards feared that cold showers might allow prisoners to become more resistant to the cold and improve their odds of escaping.

Olivia: Alcatraz is on an island in the ice-cold San Francisco Bay—it was notorious for being the hardest prison to escape from. Conditions were terrible, but it had two things going for it: good food and hot showers. The guards thought the good food would prevent riots and hot showers would prevent prisoners from acclimating to the cold, making an escape attempt harder.

Josie: Olivia, did you know that there was an inmate at Alcatraz who became a respected ornithologist in prison? He raised birds and wrote a book on canaries—the book had to be smuggled out to be published. He even found a cure for a common canary disease. Eventually, prison guards took away his birds and he died in prison, having spent most of his life in solitary confinement.

M: *The fact that his book had to be smuggled out says a lot about our priorities as a society.*

The largest extinction in Earth's history was the Permian extinction, where 90 percent of all living species on the planet died—possibly due to global warming fueled by volcanic eruptions.

Lloyd: And that's just one of the five mass extinctions in Earth's history.

Izzy: Fingers crossed there's not a sixth anytime soon.

Lloyd: The way things are going, I wouldn't be so sure!

M: Scientists disagree on what qualifies as an "extinction event." Some estimate there have been as many as 20 extinction events!

During the Bronze Age Collapse, multiple major civilizations collapsed within a short period of time in the twelfth century BCE. We still don't know exactly why.

Dick: It's truly one of the greatest mysteries in archaeology. A modern, interconnected Mediterranean world—some of these places with running water and toilets—imploded in just a few decades.

Adam: What about the Sea Peoples?

Dick: Well, for a while that was the dominant theory for the collapse: There was a group of invaders that seemed to ravage large parts of the Mediterranean, bringing entire cities down. But we're *still* not sure who they were.

Adam: What's the best current theory?

Dick: Some of the first cities to fall were in ancient Greece. There is a growing school of thought that those cities falling were not necessarily attacked *by* the Sea Peoples, but rather *produced* the Sea Peoples. Think about it: As these cities in Greece fell apart, it created this entire class of people who were great at combat, great at sailing, but had no economic opportunities. So, what do they do? Take to the sea. Some emigrated, some turned to piracy, some did both. As time went on, other groups of people joined them and created a sort of "pirate coalition" that became the feared Sea Peoples. This is all just a theory still—but I find it the most plausible.

Adam: Or maybe, just maybe . . . it was aliens.

Dick: I really, really don't think that was the case, Adam.

M: Boy, aliens really are such an easy explanation for anything we don't know, aren't they? But everything in history is more complex than it seems. There are rarely easy explanations, be wary of anyone who provides one. Some even argue that the Bronze Age Collapse wasn't really a "collapse"—just a redistribution of power from the elites back to the common people.

President James Garfield may have been killed by the medical treatment he received after being shot, rather than by the bullet itself.

Olivia: There's a phenomenon in medicine called "VIP syndrome," where high-status patients paradoxically get worse medical treatment than the average person, because doctors want so badly to help them. They perform experimental treatments, unnecessary procedures, and the like.

Josie: Garfield had a tough time. There was a bullet left in his body and doctors kept probing with dirty fingers to try to get it out. Alexander Graham Bell (yes, the telephone guy) invented a metal detector to find the bullet. But the doctor who was working on the president insisted that only the right side of the president's body be examined, where he thought the bullet was. Ironically, if they had checked the left side, they probably would have found the bullet. The invasive search for the bullet eventually punctured Garfield's liver. Oh, and during all this, they gave the president enemas of whiskey and beef bouillon.

Olivia: And this wasn't just a couple of days. He lived for nearly three months like that—poor guy. His last words? "This pain, this pain." Which like, fair enough. Rough time.

The ancient, 5,000-year-old Indus Valley Civilization may not have had a ruling class.

Dick: This is one of the only examples we have of a complex ancient civilization without clear evidence of an elite class. There was urbanization, advanced monument building, but apparently no elite class to organize or enforce any of this. Social stratification, from what we can see in the archaeological record, seemed minimal.

Javier: So how did they function?

Dick: It's possible that the community just came together on its own accord to build these things. The Indus Valley Civilization contradicts traditional narratives, in which the development of an elite class is a critical step on the path to development and "civilization." Some archaeologists even argue it's the first step—that civilization arises to cater to the needs of the elite, and not the other way around.

M: How do we know this? Well, we analyze class distinction in ancient societies by different proxies—for example, the goods left in different people's graves, differences in the size of houses, etc. We haven't observed much of this in the Indus Valley Civilization, so archaeologists assume there were minimal social distinctions. Of course, it's possible social distinctions just looked different, or that we're not looking in the right places.

Cave art may have had technological purpose—communicating information on migration patterns, mating cycles of animals, and other important ideas.

Josie: There are repeating symbols over thousands of years of cave art that seem to be evidence of common visual language. A recent study indicates that repeating dots that occur in many cave paintings might be an early form of calendar, tracking lunar months to identify animals' mating and migration patterns for hunting.

Izzy: There's another theory that certain cave art becomes "animated" under firelight. Flickering light and shadows create the optical illusion of movement. Who knows if it was intentional, but I think the idea of caveman cartoons is pretty damn cool!

Lloyd: Caveman anime. I like it.

M: The farther we look back in time, the harder it is to analyze meaning in symbols. But there has been some groundbreaking research on cave art, like the kind Josie and Izzy are talking about. The theories are fascinating if true!

Ancient Romans wiped their butts with a sponge on a stick and shared it with other people who used the same bathroom. It sat in a jar of vinegar between wipings.

Adam: Nah, shared wiping? I can't get behind that.

Dick: There are a few archaeologists who argue that we've misinterpreted the evidence, and those sponges were actually used for cleaning the bathroom itself.

Adam: I sure hope that's true, for the Romans' sake.

Dick: Pretty smart of them to use vinegar as a disinfectant—especially since they didn't even know that germs existed!

Adam: Yeah, but the same people put lead in their wine so, you know, you can't win 'em all.

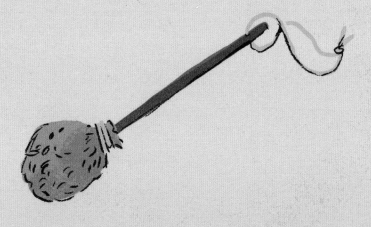

The ancient Greeks used to wipe their butts with the names of their enemies.

Dick: They'd use discarded pieces of clay pots, known as ostraca. They'd use these same ostraca to vote someone out of their town, which might be where the word ostracize comes from. They'd literally wipe their asses with the names of their enemies.

Olivia: You know, I can get behind that.

M: Doesn't sound very comfortable though. And you'd need to be VERY careful to avoid sharp edges!

People in ancient Japan wiped their butts with *kan-shiketsu,* which translates from Japanese to "dry shit stick." People in China used a similar approach.

Olivia: Do you think they got more or fewer splinters than the folks using early toilet paper?

Josie: Don't remind me, I'll keep my splinter-free toilet paper.

M: At least they didn't share it, like the Romans.

The deadliest part of pre-modern battles was usually the retreat.

Dick: One of the strange things about ancient combat is that we don't know *exactly* how it happened. Think about this—if I were writing a book today, I might say, "he opened a can of soda," because everyone knows what that means. But a thousand years from now, they might wonder: "How does one open a can of soda? Does one cut it open? Does one pierce it with a hammer?"

Olivia: You really think so?

Dick: Well, sure. It would be strange to write: "He slid his finger under the metal tab of the can, which built pressure so the perforated circle on top of the can split open and created a hole from which the sweet carbonated beverage could be drank." In the same way, ancient authors wrote, "The two armies collided" or, "He slew five men." But the physical mechanics of how armies crashed into each other—what that physical combat looked like—is actually hotly debated. The image you probably have in your head right now is more Hollywood than history.

Olivia: Damn.

Dick: But there is one thing we know: on the day of the battle, most people died in retreat. And this was true up until, and sometimes including, very recently. As long as an army could hold its mettle and hold the line, deaths occurred rather slowly. But once morale broke and the retreat started, panic set in—and that's when most deaths occurred. "Every man for himself" was, ironically, the surest way to die.

Adam: That's one of the reasons why more professional armies were so much more effective in pre-modern times. They had the experience and mettle to hold formation, which is half the battle. They could often defeat armies much larger than themselves if they had the patience and grit to resist panicking. I mean, hell, I get it. Can't judge 'em. I panic about writing an email sometimes! I can't imagine staring down a screaming barbarian covered in paint and blood—I'd probably piss myself and run, too!

Olivia: I wouldn't. I'm built different!

Dick: Olivia, you get nervous ordering pizza on the phone.

Olivia: Fair point.

Dessert

M: Well, if all this potty talk hasn't ruined your appetite, I hope you saved room for dessert! We have an incredible spread. Coconut panna cotta, baked Alaska, apple tart, and chocolate mousse. Take your pick, eat them all, or just have a bite. I also have a tasty dessert wine—some Icewine. The grapes freeze on the vine and it concentrates the sugar, making for a delicious, sweet wine.

I think in some respects, our brains are the same way. It's only by being exposed to challenging ideas that our thoughts and beliefs crystalize in more meaningful ways. And our lives become sweeter because of it.

How are you enjoying yourself? I told you this was a strange bunch of people who love to talk about strange things! Do you feel smarter yet? Well, you'll certainly have plenty to talk about at the next party you attend. But hold on to your seat, because we're just getting started with the really crazy stuff!

During Prohibition, the US government put poison in illicit booze and killed up to 10,000 people.

Izzy: How much do you have to hate booze to think that killing people is a better alternative to them having a whiskey and Coke?

Olivia: And then when they repealed Prohibition they were just like, "Oops, my bad, it's legal now." No apologies or reparations to those people's families or anything.

Izzy: Meanwhile, bootleggers made money hand over fist.

Adam: There's actually a whole economic theory called "Bootleggers and Baptists" that describes how criminals make hella money from prohibition. Sometimes criminals even support those policies because they limit competition. It's all supply and demand.

M: Thank goodness Prohibition is over, because this Icewine is delicious!

The pharmaceutical company Bayer invented heroin.

Olivia: The people who make aspirin?

Izzy: Yup, same people. Think about it—it's the same naming convention. Aspir-in. Hero-in. They released it as a pain reliever and cough suppressant.

Olivia: A *cough suppressant?* How bad does your cough need to be to take heroin for it?

Izzy: You know what Bayer also manufactured? The gas used in the Holocaust. Well, not them exactly, but a subsidiary company. And they tested drugs in concentration camps. But that's not suitable conversation over dessert, is it?

Olivia: No, I suppose not. Maybe best to have another slice of apple tart and move on!

M: Bayer has a very complicated history.

The CIA dosed hundreds of people with LSD without their consent during the 1950s and '60s.

Olivia: Alright, come on, that's gotta just be a wacky conspiracy theory, right?

Adam: More like conspiracy fact. There was a congressional hearing about the MKUltra program in 1977, and the US government declassified thousands of pages of material on it. The CIA didn't try to hide it—they bragged about it!

Olivia: Okay, tell me about it.

Adam: Well, LSD was first synthesized in 1938. It's a highly hallucinogenic drug, and our government wondered if we could use it for interrogation as a truth serum. Or even as some form of mind control.

Izzy: Which is ironic because "control" is the last word I'd use to describe what it feels like to take it!

Adam: The CIA was really wild back then. They built a brothel with one-way mirrors on the wall and hired prostitutes to bring customers in and dose them with LSD. The CIA watched through the mirrors. They also dosed their own employees randomly—it was almost a "prank" for some of them. They even dosed prisoners and psychiatric patients. Hell, they gave LSD to one patient for *174 days straight*.

Izzy: In my very educated opinion as a psychologist, that is distinctly not a good idea.

Adam: But it gets even stranger. The CIA may have accidentally invented the hippie movement. Or at least contributed to it. You see, author Ken Kesey was an all-American boy in college. He played football and didn't drink. And he was patriotic! So patriotic, in fact, that he signed up for a voluntary CIA study to "help his country." During the study, they gave him LSD in a hospital room and observed him for the next 12 hours. Surprisingly, he had a great time. And wanted more.

He ended up being a major figure in the early hippie movement. He wrote *One Flew Over the Cuckoo's Nest* and held parties known as "Acid Tests" in San Francisco where he gave everyone LSD (consensually, as opposed to the CIA). This is where the Grateful Dead got their start, as well as the Merry Pranksters, the people who popularized tie-dye. It was, in some ways, the beginning of the hippie movement, or at the very least steroids for its growth.

Izzy: Serves the CIA right, I suppose, for messing with people like that. If we did that stuff in another country, it would be a war crime!

M: I can't lie, pretty much everything Adam mentioned is not only true but documented in Senate trials. Sometimes, rarely, conspiracy theories are actually just conspiracy facts! MKUltra might just be the weirdest thing in American history.

There are sharks older than the United States of America.

Josie: Greenland sharks are the longest-living vertebrates we know about. They live for over 250 years, and possibly as long as 500 years—twice as long as the United States has been a country!

Olivia: And they eat them in Iceland in that fermented dish! Have you tried it?

Josie: I have. *Hákarl*, they call it. I visited Iceland a few years back. It tastes . . . very bad in my opinion. But that's because the shark's meat is poisonous, and the fermentation process breaks down the toxins. The flesh has a high urea content, which makes it taste like piss. Literally. It's the same chemical. But it's pretty darn amazing that they discovered how to break down those toxins so long ago!

Olivia: People find a way to get by everywhere, I suppose.

M: If you go to Iceland, don't try it. It's horrible. Value your self-worth, my friend!

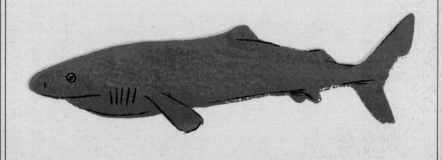

Coca-Cola (with cocaine) was invented as a "healthier" alternative to another beverage.

Izzy: There was a very popular drink in the late 1800s, particularly in France, called Vin Mariani. It was wine mixed with cocaine. Now, you have to understand—this was *insanely* popular. Thomas Edison drank it and said it helped him stay awake. Ulysses S. Grant drank it while writing his memoirs. Pope Leo XIII appeared in an advertisement for it and awarded a Vatican gold medal to the inventor for creating such a *delectable* beverage.

Olivia: It was like an old-school version of Four Loko, huh?

Izzy: Yeah, basically. Because it was so popular, John Pemberton, this guy in Georgia, invents a competitor and adds a third ingredient: kola nuts for caffeine. So now it is wine plus cocaine plus caffeine. Even stronger.

Javier: Ah yes, exactly what that drink needed, another stimulant!

Izzy: But then John Pemberton's county in Georgia passed prohibition laws. So Pemberton removed the wine from his drink. What is he left with? A beverage made from coca leaves . . . and kola nuts. Coca and kola. Coca-Cola.

Javier: Wow, so people were like, "I'm so healthy, I'm *only* drinking cocaine. No wine for me please!"

Izzy: Literally. It was marketed as a healthy beverage!

M: I suppose everything is relative! I wonder what people in the future will think of the things we eat and drink today.

One strain of the common cold may have come from camels.

Josie: A 2016 study showed that one of the viruses that causes the common cold very likely originated in camels before being passed on to humans.

Lloyd: That's one reason people are so afraid of MERS. It's a deadly camel-borne coronavirus that's already killed over 800 people. We're pretty fortunate that every outbreak has been contained so far.

M: The common cold can be caused by over 200 different viruses, but is mostly due to different types of rhinoviruses and coronaviruses.

In the United Kingdom, a 1986 law made it illegal to handle salmon in suspicious circumstances.

Olivia: How many times did this happen that they had to make a whole *law* for it?

M: Many of these "crazy laws" are funny interpretations of real laws. This was a law that was actually intended to stop salmon poaching. There are loads of apocryphal laws. For example, there's a popular myth that it's illegal to throw a moose out of a plane in Alaska. Whenever a fact sounds "too good to be true," remember: there are many different ways to frame the same information. The most compelling way is often the one that ends up being repeated!

GPS satellites need to change their clocks to account for Einstein's theory of relativity.

Lloyd: The stronger the influence of gravity, the slower time moves. That's why sci-fi movies show time slowing down near black holes: because black holes have such strong gravitational pull.

Izzy: I'm confused.

Lloyd: Therefore, time moves *faster* at higher elevations—because there is less influence of gravity. Since satellites are farther from Earth, the pull of gravity is weaker up there, so time is 38 microseconds faster on those satellites than on Earth.

Izzy: Nope. I don't like that fact one bit. Makes me too existential.

Time moves faster for your head than your feet.

Lloyd: Because your feet are closer to Earth than your head, they experience more gravity and therefore slower time. This might sound purely hypothetical, but in 2010, scientists took two atomic clocks and put one 12 inches (30 centimeters) above the other. And they *could* actually calculate the difference in time. Even by just a foot.

Izzy: Alright, now I'm spiraling.

Lloyd: Just wait until you find out why this happens: because gravity literally warps space-time!

M: That also means time moves faster in high-altitude cities, like Denver, than in sea-level cities, like New Orleans.

People used to think that disease was caused by "night air." They made sure to close all windows at nighttime.

Josie: It's called "miasma theory." You know, I always wondered how much of that was because of mosquito-borne illness. If you're in an area with a lot of malaria (and the United States and Europe had plenty of malaria back in the day), closing your windows makes sense. The word "malaria" even comes from Italian—it means "bad air."

Javier: It's also where Buenos Aires gets its name, because it is one of the first cities on the way down the South American coast that doesn't have malaria. So it was named Buenos Aires, "good airs."

Lloyd: People also thought that smelly air carried disease—which makes sense considering how bad cities used to smell. But ironically, some of their solutions for "miasma" actually worked. For example, in the mid-1800s, London upgraded its water and sewage systems to try to get rid of bad smells and stop cholera epidemics. People at that time didn't really understand what caused disease. And yet, the intervention worked, because—shocker—clean water and better sewage disposal means less cholera!

M: It's like when you use the wrong formula but still get the right answer.

The United States got rid of malaria by spraying DDT everywhere.

Josie: Okay, that's a little bit of an exaggeration, but not by much. The United States used to have a serious malaria problem, especially in wetland areas, like the South and even Washington, DC.

Olivia: So what did we do?

Josie: Well, after World War II, there was the National Malaria Eradication Program, which basically translated to: kill every mosquito that carries malaria. Not every species of mosquito carries malaria, just the genus *Anopheles*.

Olivia: But how did we kill them all?

Josie: With *a lot* of poison. Over four million applications. Was it incredibly toxic? Yes. Did it damage the ecosystem? Yes. But did we get rid of malaria? Also yes. Was it worth it? Maybe.

M: That "maybe" is doing a lot of work.

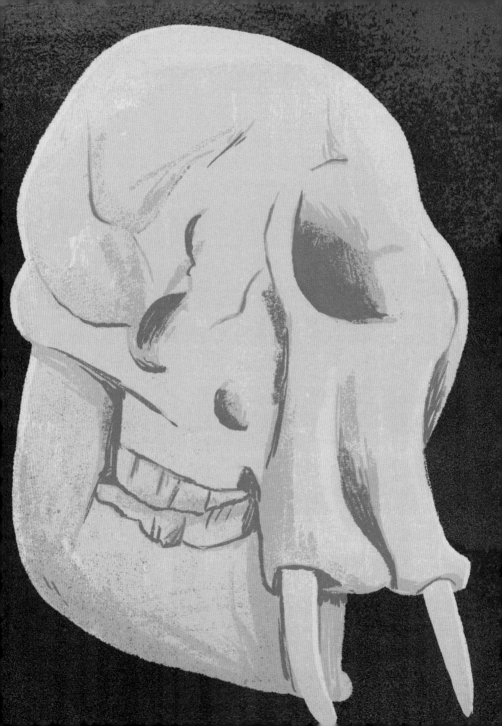

It is possible that the ancient myth of the "Cyclops" was inspired by skulls of dwarf elephants found on Cyprus.

Dick: This is *just* a theory and we have no proof—but look at how Cyclopean these skulls look. They come from a species of Mediterranean elephant that went extinct, and its nasal cavity looks quite a bit like an eye socket. So I'll let you make your own assumptions, chap.

Adam: I always wonder how many myths must have come from fossil finds in the past. Like, ancient humans *must* have discovered dinosaur fossils, at least accidentally. Surely that made their imaginations run!

M: At least Adam didn't think it was aliens! Don't forget the dwarf elephant theory is just that—a theory with no concrete evidence. Establishing causality that far back in the past can be tricky business. Some scientists even think the myth may have been inspired by mammoth skulls further inland.

Because every day is not the same length, scientists sometimes need to add a "leap second" to a year to keep clocks accurate.

Lloyd: Lots of things influence how long it takes the Earth to rotate— friction from tides, and even earthquakes. As a matter of fact, a 2011 earthquake in Japan shortened the length of the day by 1.8 microseconds.

Javier: How many leap seconds have we had?

Lloyd: Since we started counting in the '70s, there have been 27 leap seconds. That's almost half a leap minute!

M: Well, I certainly feel like MY days are getting longer.

A newborn baby panda is the size of a mouse when it's born.

Josie: Pandas are herbivores. One theory is that their diet is not particularly nutrient-dense, so they have to make smaller babies. Pregnant mothers don't have as much extra nutrition to spare.

Dick: Take that, vegans!

Josie: A newborn panda is 900 times smaller than its mother. If humans had the same ratio, adult humans would weigh as much as a Ford F-250 truck.

Izzy: I want to pet one! Their fur looks so soft.

M: I don't want to burst Izzy's bubble, but panda hair is actually coarse and scratchy, like raw sheep's wool.

Before alarm clocks, "knocker-upper" was a profession. People would go door-to-door and knock or shoot pebbles at your window to make noise.

Izzy: But who woke *them* up? Was there a whole pyramid scheme of knocker-uppers all the way down?

Olivia: Who knocks up the knocker-upper?

Izzy: Well, hopefully the knocker-upper's husband!

Olivia: Oh, I didn't mean it like that!

M: Get your head out of the gutter!

Many arctic explorers died of scurvy despite being surrounded by sources of vitamin C.

Josie: There was a recent study on Inuit diets. There's always been this big question: How do Inuit people not get scurvy? You get scurvy from a lack of vitamin C, and it's not like there are a whole bunch of lemons and limes growing in the Arctic.

Dick: That's also how British people became referred to as "Limeys"— their sailors used to travel with stocks of limes to prevent scurvy on long voyages.

Josie: Well, ain't no limes in the Arctic. Some of the vitamin C in an Inuit diet comes from raw meat. When you cook meat, the vitamin C degrades, so raw meat has a bit more. But most of it comes from algae they harvest from the water.

Dick: Which means that sailors died surrounded by the very algae that could have saved them. How poetic.

M: Algae, algae everywhere and not a drop to eat.

Clownfish are sequential hermaphrodites, which means they transition from male to female over the course of their lives.

Josie: Even cooler than that—when a male clownfish turns into a female, she becomes the leader of a whole pack of males. And when that female dies, the second-in-command male becomes a female and takes her place.

Olivia: That's some girlboss energy right there.

Josie: Clownfish are wild. Their eggs hatch during full moons or new moons because that's when tides are the highest. Those swift tides protect hatchlings from predators. How do they even know when to do that? It's crazy.

Olivia: We stan clownfish.

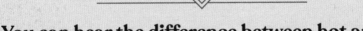

You can hear the difference between hot and cold water pouring.

Izzy: We can tell the difference consistently. Just think for a minute about the sound of pouring hot tea versus an ice-cold glass of water. It's different, isn't it? One is lower pitch, the other higher. Scientists aren't 100 percent sure why this is, but it probably has something to do with the viscosity of the water being affected by temperature. Hot water is less viscous—it flows more quickly.

M: Gosh, I wish you could listen to this right now. You'll just have to imagine, I suppose! Or even better, test it yourself.

In the Yucatán Peninsula, there is a tradition of using living bejeweled makech beetles as accessories.

Olivia: Slay.

Josie: I don't know how I feel about that, it doesn't seem like the most ethical thing in the world.

Olivia: I don't know, maybe the beetles are happy.

M: One must imagine Sisyphus happy.

"Cute aggression" is the observed phenomenon that, when some people see something cute, they want to smush it, pinch it, or devour it.

Izzy: It also translates into language when people say things like "I could just eat you up!" to a baby. It's really strange when you think about these kinds of remarks out of context!

M: I've never thought about that, but it is rather strange, isn't it?

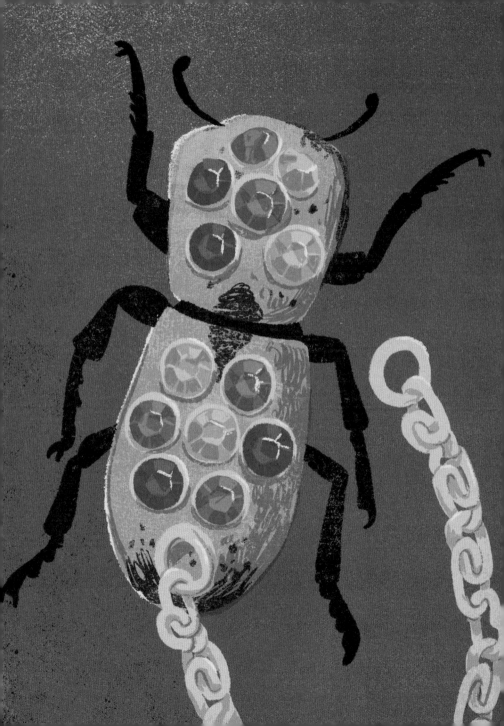

Chimpanzees have been observed engaging in war

Josie: This is one of the craziest stories I know. Jane Goodall, the famous scientist who studied chimpanzees, saw a multi-year civil war among a group of chimpanzees. They were once all best friends, but after the leader died, there was a power struggle and they split into north and south groups. For four years, they engaged in constant conflict, killing the creatures they had once lived with.

Dick: Sounds very human to me so far.

Josie: They used war strategies. Groups of males raided opposition territory to kill enemies. They were observed celebrating, howling, and throwing branches after beating their enemies to death. The northern group ended up winning, killing all the opposing males of the south. But then something even more human happened—it turns out the southern group had been a kind of "buffer state." Without it, other chimpanzee communities were free to attack the northern group. Really feels like human geopolitics!

Dick: Rousseau would be rolling in his grave. "Noble savage," indeed.

Josie: Goodall said she was never the same. Before, she had assumed the chimps were "rather nicer" than human beings. But for years after, she had nightmares about the chimpanzee violence and cruelty she had witnessed.

Dick: Wait until she sees humans!

M: For years, people thought human intervention had caused this, but other studies disproved that theory. Turns out, chimps just go to war. Don't let them get tanks!

The "mystery" disappearance of people from Roanoke Island, North Carolina, has likely been solved.

Olivia: More than 100 American colonists disappeared from Roanoke Island, leaving only a single word carved into a tree: "CROATOAN." For years, people wondered what happened to them. Was it aliens? Was it starvation? Were they murdered by the Croatoan tribe (hence, the carving)?

Adam: Maybe they were time travelers.

Olivia: The research seems to point to a simpler answer: they fully integrated with the Croatoan tribe. New research shows strong evidence of mixed communities thriving for generations, with varied diets indicative of a surplus of food! They even tried to tell everyone where they went: "Croatoan." But the European imagination of the time assumed it was more likely they were killed by the Croatoans than hanging out with them! There were even blue-eyed descendants of the tribe generations later.

M: This topic is still debated, but broadly the evidence seems to point to Olivia being correct.

Paul Revere, the famous figure from the American Revolution, was a part-time dentist.

Adam: Boston Tea Party, hold the sugar.

M: George Washington's dentures were made with lead and possibly included the teeth of enslaved people, so dentistry was a little different back then.

During the American Revolution, British soldiers formed military theatrical companies and performed on American stages.

Adam: It was mostly to alleviate the boredom of occupation, but also as a propaganda tool. They did a bit of Shakespeare as well. Men often played women's roles back then, so these big British soldiers would have been on American stages performing in dresses.

Olivia: Maybe that's the reason for the Third Amendment—Americans didn't want to quarter soldiers because they were theater kids!

M: It's funny how some amendments are broad and timeless (like free speech), and others feel so specific to the time period. They were mad about housing British soldiers and made an entire amendment about it.

Pluto has about the same surface area as Russia.

Olivia: I was sad when they said Pluto wasn't a planet anymore. I feel like I'm missing a part of my childhood.

Lloyd: Well, it's a dwarf planet still, if that makes you feel any better.

M: I don't know if Pluto is smaller than I expected or if Russia is bigger!

Roman Emperor Caligula wanted to make his horse a senator and may have fed him oats mixed with gold flakes.

Izzy: He was probably just horsing around.

Josie: He was tired of all the horseplay in the Senate.

Izzy: He just wanted to upset his *neigh*bors.

Josie: Everyone was in a rush, so he told them to hold their horses.

Izzy: He was champing at the bit to do it.

Dick: You all know that's probably a myth, right? Ancient historians may have made it up to make Caligula look worse—or it may have been mostly symbolic.

Olivia: Oh, don't be a party pooper, Dick. We'll try to . . . rein it in!

Dick: I can't with you guys.

Olivia: You're right, though. At this point we're just beating a dead horse.

M: If these bad puns keep up, I'm gonna have to hoof it out of here.

Pope Benedict IX was the only man to ever be pope more than once. He was also the youngest pope and the only person to ever sell the papacy.

Javier: This was a very corrupt time—*que corrupto*. He was elected when he was 20 because his father paid a huge bribe. Supposedly he was forced out of the papacy due to his depraved lifestyle. But then, he came back for the sequel! When he was pope again, he decided he wanted to marry his cousin, so he *sold* the papacy to someone else. Then, he changed his mind a third time and came back to finish the trilogy, becoming pope once more. He was also related to six other popes.

M: Related to six popes? Definitely a nepo baby.

During the American Revolution, George Washington mandated that all his troops be inoculated against smallpox to prevent an outbreak.

Adam: Even back then, it was controversial. Some of his generals prohibited the inoculation, and later, their troops had smallpox outbreaks that put total troop numbers at risk.

M: Smallpox was a horrific way to die. I'm grateful we eradicated it—truly one of mankind's greatest achievements.

The human body has enough iron in it to make a two-inch (five-centimeter) iron nail.

Izzy: Don't tell the robots that or AI might start harvesting us for computer building materials!

Dick: Fortunately, there's plenty of iron in the world to go around.

Izzy: Okay good, because if this world becomes like *The Matrix*, I'm taking the blue pill. Keep me in the simulation! I'll take the beer and steak, even if it's fake.

M: Isn't it wild that The Matrix *was a movie about how terrible it was to have an office job with a livable income in the '90s? Neo's life sounds pretty good these days!*

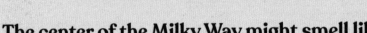

The center of the Milky Way might smell like rum and taste like raspberries.

Adam: By "Milky Way," do you mean the candy bar?

Lloyd: No, Adam, we're talking about the galaxy. At the center of the Milky Way there is a giant dust cloud called Sagittarius B2, and we've detected a substance called ethyl formate there. *That* is the chemical that gives raspberries their characteristic flavor. And on its own, it smells like rum.

Adam: I volunteer as an astronaut to go there! Sounds delicious.

M: Unfortunately, the same dust cloud also contains propyl cyanide, which is lethal. So maybe leave the space helmet on.

As a student, English poet Lord Byron was so upset about his university banning students from having dogs that he brought a tame bear to his dorm.

Javier: Lord Byron was a weirdo, he drank out of skulls. His daughter is also famous: Ada Lovelace, the woman who invented computer programming.

M: Separating history from myth is tough with figures like Byron. An undoubtedly eccentric and successful family, though!

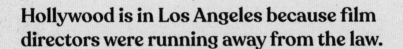

Hollywood is in Los Angeles because film directors were running away from the law.

Javier: This is a fact *increíble*. Thomas Edison and his cronies owned all the patents for making movies at the beginning of the twentieth century. And I mean ALL of them. So it was incredibly expensive to make a movie—you had to pay these guys for the camera, the film, the lighting, everything.

Dick: If there's one thing Edison knew how to do, it was how to make money.

Javier: But his patents were filed in New Jersey. So a bunch of film producers had the idea to go as far away from New Jersey as possible—across the country, to the middle of the desert, to an area today known as Hollywood. They started making movies in California and hoped that Edison's lawyers wouldn't find them.

M: I suppose Hollywood has never been particularly known for its morals.

Iceland may have the world's oldest surviving parliament. It first convened in 930 CE.

Javier: I can't look at Icelandic people the same way after learning how they make fermented shark.

Josie: Iceland has a unique culture. They were so isolated for so long they kind of just did their own thing.

M: *The entire population of Iceland is smaller than that of Tulsa, Oklahoma.*

Brussels Airport sells more chocolate to consumers than anywhere else on the planet.

Olivia: It makes sense, Belgian chocolate is super famous. And everyone visiting wants to buy some to take back to their family. The airport sells two METRIC TONS of chocolate per day. That's over 4,000 pounds of chocolate a day or 3.3 pounds of chocolate every minute. Yum!

M: *Pretty ironic considering cocoa doesn't even grow in Belgium. The country is famous for chocolate because of an ugly colonial past—but we won't get into that over dessert.*

Shakespeare contributed about 1,700 words to the English language.

Olivia: Shakespeare's writings have the first recorded usage of words like *downstairs, undress, lonely, bedroom*—you'll notice in a lot of these, he's combining two words or altering an existing word.

Dick: But here's the rub, honey: we're not sure whether he invented these words, or whether he was just the first to write them down. Shakespeare was famous for using vernacular English and speaking to the common man.

Olivia: Which is ironic, since today he's thought to be so fancy.

Dick: But in his own time, his plays were kind of lowbrow. People showed up, likely drunk, and for a penny they could stand on the ground in front of the stage and watch the show. They called that part of the audience "groundlings."

Olivia: Shakespeare didn't just invent words, he invented whole phrases, too. *In a pickle, wild goose chase, all that glitters isn't gold*—so many of the idioms we use today come from Shakespeare.

M: Pretty crazy those words and phrases have survived almost half a millennium. I wonder what authors will still be read 400 years from now.

The Mongol Empire may have killed up to 10 percent of the world's population at the time.

Javier: Wow. They killed one in every ten people? That is hard to believe.

Dick: It's the truth. Also, one in every 200 men in the world is related to Genghis Khan. Being the biggest empire in world history has lasting consequences.

Javier: It's odd—if Genghis Khan or Alexander the Great had lived more recently, we'd consider them genocidal maniacs. But when enough time passes, they become historical figures and people even admire them.

M: Dick is wrong about the size of the Mongol Empire here—he's conveniently forgetting the British Empire. It was 50 percent larger. At its height, the British Empire covered a quarter of the world's land.

Humans can smell rain better than sharks can smell blood.

Josie: The smell of the ground after it rains is known as petrichor, and it's caused by a chemical called geosmin. The human nose is insanely sensitive to geosmin—we only need a few molecules per TEN BILLION molecules of air to detect it.

Lloyd: Why are we so sensitive to it?

Josie: Well, that's where things get interesting, Lloyd. We're not sure. Some scientists believe it's a survival mechanism—evolution selected for our ability to find fresh water. Places where it recently rained are a pretty good bet for clean water and food.

Lloyd: That makes sense.

Josie: But it could also be random. Humans are also incredibly sensitive to the smell of vanillin, the organic compound found in vanilla beans. Was finding vanilla a huge survival advantage? Probably not, unless cavemen really loved cupcakes. But the same receptors that detect vanillin can also detect high heat, which is a very important thing for not dying!

The average human eye can see the equivalent of 576 megapixels.

Lloyd: That's about equivalent to the resolution of 48 iPhones.

Izzy: But that number doesn't tell the whole story—our eyes need to move around to map those 576 megapixels. Most of our field of vision is peripheral, so a single "snapshot" of our vision is closer to 5 to 15 megapixels: about the same as an iPhone camera.

M: I can SEE her point.

During World War I, France built a decoy of Paris to confuse bombers.

Adam: This is actually a crazy fact. During World War I, France had an idea to prevent Paris from being bombed. They built a decoy city about 15 miles (24 kilometers) away from the real one. They created entire neighborhoods, made copies of famous monuments (like the Arc de Triomphe), and even hired the guy who lit the Eiffel Tower to design lighting for the city.

Javier: Wow, that's a ridiculous amount of effort. Did it work?

Adam: Kind of. This was before radar and missile defense systems. Pilots' navigation was more rudimentary. At night, they turned off all the lights in the real Paris, but left a few dim ones on in fake Paris. They wanted to make it look like the people there were trying to keep their lights off but failing. It was brilliant, in a way.

M: *The French built a fake city in World War I, but surrendered within six weeks during World War II. How times change.*

Martin Luther King Jr.'s birth name was Michael King. When he was five, his dad changed both of their names to Martin Luther in honor of the famous German priest who kicked off the Protestant Reformation.

Dick: I wonder if he would have been as famous with a different name.

Izzy: I'm sure he would. "A rose by any other name . . ."

Dick: The name Michael King sounds too much like Michael Caine to me.

Adam: Funny you should say that—Michael Caine wasn't the actor's real name, either. HIS real name is Maurice Joseph Micklewhite.

Dick: Wow, that is . . . um, much less cool. Much less suave. I see why he changed it.

M: And Vin Diesel's real name is Mark Sinclair. Sounds like a Victorian author, or maybe an oil baron.

The 15-foot-tall mosaics inside Cinderella Castle at Walt Disney World were created by a former Nazi interrogator.

Izzy: Not just any Nazi, either. Hanns Scharff was *the* top Nazi interrogator during World War II.

Adam: I've heard of this guy. After the war, the United States let him immigrate so he could help the government and teach interrogation techniques. The US military still learns some of his methods today, apparently.

Izzy: He's famous for using psychological interrogation. He kind of pioneered "good cop, bad cop"—he'd befriend prisoners, or offer them food, things like that. And then after the war, in an utterly bizarre turn of events, he started a mosaic company in America that became extremely successful. Like, this guy was one of the best mosaic makers in America—that's why Disney hired him.

Javier: I don't know how I feel about the fact that they just let a top Nazi immigrate to America, no problem.

Izzy: Well, they let Nazi rocket scientists into America—and they helped us get to the moon!

Javier: But that's different. Those were men of science. Hanns Scharff was interrogating prisoners. That feels worse, somehow.

M: *Hanns Scharff's mosaics currently reside in Los Angeles City Hall, Cinderella Castle, Epcot, and the University of Southern California.*

The World War I's Battle of Verdun, which took place in northeast France, was so brutal that the area is still uninhabitable today, over 100 years later.

Dick: They call it the *Zone Rouge*, or the Red Zone. There's so much unexploded ordnance that it is completely unlivable. The ground still has craters from the explosions.

Adam: There were 750,000 casualties at the Battle of Verdun. That's more than the population of the city of Seattle—in a single battle.

Dick: But it's still not the deadliest battle in history. That would be Stalingrad, during World War II—1.2 million casualties in a single battle.

M: Keep in mind, when someone says casualties, that includes both dead and wounded. Always ask for definitions when you hear statistics. Still a ludicrous number, though!

Canadians say "sorry" so frequently that they passed bills that state an apology isn't a legal admission of guilt.

Adam: The Apology Act! I guess they were trying to prevent people who were just being polite from going to jail.

M: Fun fact: Canada also has the longest coastline of any country in the world.

The rise of the modern restaurant was largely the result of the French Revolution.

Izzy: When France went and chopped the head off ol' Louis XVI, there was an unintended consequence: a lot of out-of-work people with a set of very specific skills. All the best cooks in France worked in private kitchens for royalty. When there was no more royalty, they had to make a living somehow, and some of the first modern restaurants with menus opened.

Dick: It's funny, fine dining is viewed as so elitist now, but at the time the idea that all you needed was money (as opposed to noble blood) to eat somewhere was actually quite democratic.

M: We sometimes forget how restricted life used to be for non-noble people.

Madame Tussaud (of wax museum fame) made death masks of guillotined heads in the French Revolution.

Dick: Death masks were a very popular way to remember people. Directly after death, you'd make a mold of the person's face. Tussaud claimed in her memoir that, during the French Revolution, she would take impressions of bloody heads at actual execution sites.

Izzy: Death masks were popular—both for sculpture making and just to view the wax mask itself. Tussaud even had a death mask of Marie Antoinette.

M: Let them eat wax!

More than 70 percent of all decommissioned ships are broken down on just three beaches in South Asia.

Olivia: It's really pretty horrible—some of the worst working conditions anywhere in the world. There are these massive shipbreaking yards, where people break down ships into scrap metal. There isn't enough protection for them, it's challenging, painful work, and the chemicals are dangerous as well!

Josie: I've seen photos of shipbreaking beaches—the scale is kind of hard to comprehend. I mean, some of the larger ships are like small floating cities. Think about how hard it must be to break down a cruise ship piece by piece.

In America, leaving without saying goodbye is often referred to as an "Irish exit" or an "Irish goodbye." In the UK, it is a "French exit." And in France, it is *"filer à l'anglaise,"* to leave the English way.

Izzy: And in Germany, it's a "Polish exit!"

Dick: That's ironic because the Germans seem to love entering Poland.

Izzy: Ouch. Too soon?

M: I know a mosaic they might like!

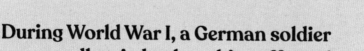

During World War I, a German soldier supposedly tried to heat his coffee using flamethrower fuel. The resulting explosion and fire killed over 600 soldiers.

Adam: Of course that's tragic, but I mean . . . what exactly did they expect?

M: Hey, I get it. I'm useless before I've had my morning coffee, too.

In 1914, during World War I, the German army caught France unprepared, and so France requisitioned more than 600 taxis from Paris to transport troops to the front. The drivers left their meters running and the government paid them normal taxi fares.

Lloyd: I guess it was like the opposite of Dunkirk, huh? Trying to get closer to the enemy instead of farther away.

M: The taxis could only drive 15 miles per hour (24 kilometers per hour), but it was still faster than walking. The French stopped the Germans just 40 miles (64 kilometers) outside of Paris.

Hanukkah is traditionally considered a minor Jewish holiday. Its importance increased because of its proximity to Christmas.

Izzy: Holidays seem to be flexible things—just like Christmas took on pagan aspects to compete with pagan holidays, Hanukkah tried to compete with Christmas. Basically, some Jewish parents didn't want their kids to feel left out of the holiday season, so Hanukkah started to be a little more "Christmas-like" with more gifts and all.

M: As long as you save me a latke, I don't care!

Stephen Hawking hosted a time travelers party. He invited all the guests only after the party ended. No one attended.

Javier: So either time travel is not real, or time travelers think Stephen Hawking's parties are lame.

M: If a time traveler arrives early, does that actually make them late?

In his early thirties, Julius Caesar felt like he hadn't accomplished anything.

Dick: There is this amazing story: Julius Caesar is in his early thirties, he's campaigning in Spain, and he sees a statue of Alexander the Great. He looks up at it and begins to weep. Through his tears, he says: "At my age, Alexander had conquered so many nations, but I have done nothing memorable."

Olivia: Which is ironic considering that, in over 20 languages, *Caesar* is the root of their word for emperor. *Caesar* was originally pronounced like *kaiser*, and it's where the similar-sounding German word for emperor comes from. It's also where we get *tsar* in Russian, *czar* in Hungarian, *cesarz* in Polish, *keizer* in Dutch, *keisari* in Finnish . . . the list goes on and on. Oh, and *kayser* in Turkish!

Dick: After the Ottomans conquered Constantinople in 1453, they referred to their rulers as *kayser-I Rûm*: literally "Caesar of Rome." This is because, to them, the Eastern Roman Empire (or the Byzantine Empire) was still Rome. Even some of the common people in the Ottoman Empire even called themselves *Rūmī*—Romans.

Olivia: The Roman Empire is a bit of a Ship of Theseus, isn't it? Its definition changes so much over time depending on who is looking at it. We think of the Byzantine Empire as this separate thing from the OG Roman Empire, but the people that lived there probably didn't. Even the Ottomans saw it as a continuation of ancient Rome— it's bizarre.

The Ship of Theseus is a philosophical thought exercise. If a ship goes on a long journey, and one by one every piece of the ship is replaced, does the same ship arrive back home?

Josie: It's one of my favorite thought experiments. Especially when you consider cell turnover in the human body—what percentage of cells needs to be replaced in our bodies for us to be someone else? Your body replaces around 330 billion cells every day.

Olivia: The Ship of Theseus is an impossible question to answer. If it's a different ship, at what point does it become a different ship? When 51 percent is swapped out? 90 percent? Which plank of wood was the one that made it different? And if we can't define that, is it actually different?

M: I think about this with historical buildings. Notre-Dame cathedral had that massive fire, and now it's been restored—is it the same cathedral? Is it still Notre-Dame?

The largest soccer stadium in the world is in Pyongyang, North Korea.

Adam: After South Korea was chosen to host the 1988 Summer Olympics, North Korea felt they had to build a big stadium to compete and show off. So they built one that could hold 150,000 people.

Lloyd: Ric Flair, in my opinion, is the greatest professional wrestler of all time. He actually wrestled there in 1995. Weird, I know. It was the largest live attendance of a wrestling event in history.

M: After the event, the North Korean government tried to get Ric Flair to read a statement saying that North Korea had the capability to dominate the United States. He refused.

China created a panda-shaped solar farm to make renewable energy more appealing to young people.

Izzy: Do you think they had to cut down any panda habitat to build that?

Olivia: Oh come on, Izzy, don't be so skeptical of everything!

M: I will admit, it does look very cute from the sky.

We discovered the first "virovore"—an organism that eats only viruses—in 2022.

Josie: So you've got carnivores, right? They eat meat. And you've got herbivores—they eat plants. But virovores, organisms that can live off of viruses alone, were only discovered in 2022. Scientists isolated different microorganisms from pond water and placed them in a dish with nothing to eat but viruses. One microorganism absolutely thrived, just chowing down on those viruses: a teeny microorganism called Halteria.

Lloyd: I wonder if one day we can use those microbes to eat viruses in the human body.

Josie: Wouldn't that be amazing? No signs we're anywhere close to that right now, but a girl can dream, I suppose.

M: I wonder what medicine will look like in 100 years. Forty years ago, things like gene therapy seemed in the realm of sci-fi. Now it's completely normal.

Most men didn't wear wedding rings in the United States until the 1940s.

Olivia: It used to be a total double standard—women wore weddings rings, but men didn't.

Dick: What changed?

Olivia: Well, a combination of things—some say it was that soldiers overseas missed their families. Others say it was jewelry companies marketing in the post-war boom. Still, others say it was a material representation of a new ideal of masculine domesticity that emerged post-war—the "white picket fence" husband sort of thing. Realistically, it was probably a combination of all three.

During World War I, armies used camouflage trees to spy on enemy troop movements.

Dick: They built giant fake trees that soldiers could hide inside of. It's really amazing it worked—they even hired talented artists and sculptors to increase the believability.

Adam: I guess it's not that different from a modern deer blind that hunters use, is it?

Dick: Well, not exactly—the entire inside of the tree would often be hollow!

M: Why do so many World War I inventions sound like something out of Looney Tunes? I can just imagine Wile E. Coyote hiding inside a camouflage tree, waiting to catch the Road Runner.

Coffee

Well, that dessert was delicious, wasn't it? It was nice to get into some crazier topics. Weird military tactics, conspiracy facts, and Nazi mosaic artists—those are the sort of facts I have a sweet tooth for. I never know exactly what to do with them.

I sometimes wonder if all these facts jumbling around in my brain do me any good. But I think they must. You never know when your mind will make strange and useful connections—the inventor of Velcro, for instance, was inspired by seeing burrs from a plant stick to his dog.

It's getting late, isn't it? My goodness how this night has flown by! I do hope you'll have a cup of coffee before you go—I have tea as well, if you're not a coffee drinker.

You know something?

I never want nights like this to end. Spending time with friends, surrounded by fascinating people and conversation—there's nothing in this world I enjoy more.

If only we could talk forever.

But if we can't have forever, coffee is the next best thing.

The Vikings may have worshipped cats.

Dick: Freyja, a Norse goddess of love, fertility, and battle, drove a chariot that was pulled by two cats. Cats also show up in the archaeological record at certain ritual locations.

Adam: To be fair, I practically worship my cat, too.

M: Everyone knows Valhalla, the majestic hall of the afterlife in Norse mythology—but only some of the Vikings who died in battle got to go there and dine with Odin. Freyja got to choose others, and those soldiers went to Fólkvangr, an equally honorable afterlife full of beer and celebration. Women were even allowed in Fólkvangr.

A day on Venus is longer than a year on Venus.

Lloyd: Venus rotates on its axis slower than it revolves around the sun. It's the slowest rotating planet and it's also one of only two planets to rotate clockwise.

Javier: Why?

Lloyd: We're honestly not sure. The best theory right now is that some massive object hit it years ago and knocked it out of whack.

M: I love how sometimes legitimate scientific theories sound like something a five-year old came up with. Never forget: saying you're not sure is, ironically, a sure way to sound smart. You'll notice when very smart people talk about science, they don't say "science has proved." It is always "scientists think" or "the evidence suggests." Despite popular belief, science is a method of interrogating the world that fundamentally rejects certainty. That is why it is so useful.

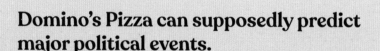

Domino's Pizza can supposedly predict major political events.

Adam: In the '90s, a guy who owned a bunch of Domino's Pizza restaurants in Washington, DC, coined the term *Pizza Meter*. It describes how journalists keep an eye on pizza orders to the CIA and the Pentagon. When orders increase, you know something is happening, because people are working late—orders supposedly doubled before the US invasion of Panama!

There are 60 seconds in a minute because the ancient Sumerians counted using base 60.

Lloyd: So, we count in base ten, right? That's why we have tens, hundreds, thousands. Everything divisible by ten. But in ancient Mesopotamia, they used a numeral system with base 60.

Dick: The first numeral system in human history! Or at least the first one written down.

Lloyd: At first, base 60 might seem completely illogical, but it has a lot of advantages. You can count to 60 with only your hands. Use your thumb to count the knuckles on one hand. Tap each knuckle with your thumb—three knuckles times four fingers equals 12. Then put a finger up on your *other* hand to symbolize 12. A second finger for 24, etc. Do that with all five fingers and you've just counted to 60 with your hands!

Olivia: Woah, that's so cool! And honestly kind of a life hack.

Dick: That really is quite handy. No pun intended.

Lloyd: Sixty is also incredibly divisible. One-third of 10 is 3.33 repeating. But one-third of 60 is 20—much easier. That's one reason why we still use base 60 for angles: 360 degrees, or six sixties.

M: We also use it for longitude and latitude. Wild that it's persisted for over 4,000 years!

The longest-running scientific experiment is the pitch drop experiment, which started in 1927 and continues to this day.

Lloyd: In 1927, a scientist wanted to demonstrate that the substance pitch (a type of asphalt) is actually liquid, even though it appears to be a solid at room temperature. In reality, it flows *very* slowly, and this scientist wanted to observe it. So he put some pitch into a funnel and waited. Sure enough, it dripped . . . years later. As a matter of fact, in 97 years, only nine drops have fallen. Ironically, each time a drop has fallen, no one has been around to witness it.

Izzy: The current experiment is now livestreamed 24/7, so we'll at least have video of the tenth drop.

M: This dark substance is also where we get the term "pitch-black" from.

The *Guinness World Records* began when a Guinness brewery manager got into an argument over the fastest game bird in Europe.

Javier: He had the idea to make the book as a promotion for Guinness, to settle arguments in pubs. Because, you know, people are always arguing about these things over a beer.

Dick: Brilliant bit of marketing, that. Same thing with the Michelin star for restaurants—it was created by the tire company. They wanted to encourage folks to take road trips (and use more tires), so they made a guide to hotels, mechanics, petrol stations, and of course: restaurants.

Javier: Makes sense how the Michelin man got so big. Too many delicious meals.

M: Ironically, I'd bet a lot of the people who break world records decide to do so after a few too many beers!

The highest mountain in our solar system is Olympus Mons. It is a volcano on Mars that is 2.5 times the height of Mount Everest.

Josie: I wanna climb it! Think about it—climbing mountains in Antarctica seemed impossible 200 years ago, and now people do it all the time. Maybe 200 years from now folks will be hiking up Olympus Mons in their space suits.

Lloyd: Olympus Mons is the size of Arizona—if you stood on top of it, you wouldn't see anything other than mountain. It's so tall that its peak is actually above the atmosphere of Mars. That means the summit is almost in a vacuum, with 2,000 times less air pressure than we experience on Earth.

Josie: But is it doable? Or is it all, like, covered in lava?

Lloyd: Well, it isn't currently erupting. At the beginning of the climb, you might have some issues with dust storms, but you'd eventually climb above them. You would need to bring a lot of oxygen, of course. That would probably be the biggest problem. And the cold! It can get down to -200°F (-129°C). But if we had sufficient advancements in technology, and, most importantly, could figure out how to GET THERE (keep in mind, we've never sent a human to Mars), then yes, I think it technically would be possible.

M: Why do I have a bad feeling that some billionaire is going to climb Olympus Mons instead of ending world hunger?

There may be more trees in Canada than there are stars in the Milky Way.

Lloyd: Believe it or not, it's incredibly hard to estimate how many stars are in the Milky Way. There are a lot of reasons for this—you can't just count them. At the center of the Milky Way is a galactic bulge filled with stars, gas, dust, and a supermassive black hole. It's so dense that we have a hard time seeing into it. So we estimate the mass of the galaxy and then try to determine what percentage of that is stars.

Izzy: So what's our current estimate?

Lloyd: Somewhere between 100 and 400 billion stars.

Izzy: That's a big range.

Lloyd: Yes, it is. And most stars are red dwarfs—which are smaller and less luminous than the sun, for example, so they can be hard to spot. But there are about 318 BILLION trees in Canada, so it's safe to say that's probably more.

M: So many measurements—particularly in outer space—are ranges and estimates. Even the number of trees in Canada is probably the middle of a reasonable range. Counting things always has some degree of sampling and estimation, so don't forget to interrogate sources and methodologies of these types of numbers.

It's possible that coffee is the reason for the Enlightenment (and therefore modern democracies).

Dick: Yes please, I'd love a cup. This is a fascinating theory by sociologist Jürgen Habermas. Coffee was introduced to Europe in the seventeenth century. At first, people thought it was medicinal, and good for "digestive issues." If you've ever had a cup of coffee on an empty stomach in the morning, I think you know exactly what kind of "digestive issues" they were talking about!

Olivia: Honey, don't be gross!

Dick: But cafés soon sprang up, becoming one of the first modern public spaces for the exchange of ideas. Before that, people had churches and alehouses—but you were too busy praying or getting drunk to talk politics. In England, they called cafés, especially those in Oxford, "penny universities," because, for the low price of a cup of coffee, you could have access to intellectual conversations, shared newspapers, and the like.

Javier: You know the company Lloyd's of London? It's one of the biggest insurance companies in the world. It started out as "Lloyd's Coffee House." It was frequented by sailors and merchants, and so many deals were being done there that Lloyd's began to sell other things to their customers, like news or insurance.

Dick: Since newspapers and pamphlets were often available to read at coffeehouses, they were almost like early libraries. On top of that, different social strata could mix in coffee houses—rich, middle class, and students all side-by-side. This, in turn, may have led to advancements in politics, academia, and even revolution.

M: *Imagine a world without coffee—it must have seemed like a miracle drug. Being caffeinated for the first time probably felt like a whole world opening up . . . Boy, this sure is good coffee, isn't it?*

A single cafe in Austria was frequented by Leon Trotsky, Adolf Hitler, and Sigmund Freud.

Dick: There's a great story from the Café Central in Vienna, likely apocryphal: the foreign minister of the Austro-Hungarian Empire was warned that a great war might spark a revolution in Russia. "And who will lead this revolution?" he said, laughing. "Perhaps Mr. Bronstein sitting over there at the Café Central?" Mr. Bronstein soon changed his name to Leon Trotsky, and the rest is history.

M: Beware of any story that fits a little too perfectly with history—George Washington chopping the cherry tree, for example. Things that are a little too perfect are often apocryphal, that means widely spread but not true. However, the very fact that we spread them often says something about the person telling it. The cherry tree story about Washington might not be true, but it may represent how Americans idolize him. Marie Antoinette never said, "Let them eat cake," but the story represents a very real disconnect between common people and the aristocracy in France at the time. Stories and facts spread because they mean something to us.

There are still six million Mayan language speakers.

Adam: What? I thought all the Mayans disappeared?

Dick: Maya. Mayan is the language family, Maya are the people. Their urban centers collapsed, but the people didn't go anywhere.

Lloyd: The Maya were so good at astronomy, they predicted a solar eclipse in 1991!

M: *The largest Maya city contained 100,000 people. That's larger than the modern-day capital of Montana.*

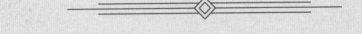

In Sweden, if you donate blood, you will receive a thank-you text when that blood is used.

Izzy: This is actually an incredibly smart way of doing things. Psychology shows us time and time again that very small incentives can shape behavior. I'd be curious to see how much blood donations increased after they started this—I'd bet quite a bit.

M: *I'd like to know where my organs go after they get donated, but I suppose that's impossible because I'll be, well, you know . . . dead.*

Ancient Egypt had their own "archaeologists" who studied even older parts of Egyptian history.

Dick: Six thousand years of history is hard to visualize. Imagine all you've learned about US history, all that you still don't know about it, and then multiply that times 30. It's tough to comprehend.

M: *The equivalent comparison would be a country that is only 8 years old compared to the USA.*

Skipper butterflies fly fast enough to compete in the Kentucky Derby.

Josie: They can reach speeds of up to 37 miles per hour (60 kilometers per hour).

Javier: That's *loco*! You're telling me butterflies could get a ticket in a school zone?

While growing, bananas go through a phase called negative geotropism. This means that instead of growing toward the ground, they start growing away from it to get closer to the sun. This is what gives them their curved shape.

Josie: Even stranger banana fact: bananas taste completely different now than they used to. We used to eat a type of banana called "Gros Michel." But in the 1950s, a fungus decimated them, so we replaced them with the hardier Cavendish banana that we eat today. It's less sweet—the original banana tasted more like how artificial banana flavoring tastes today. It was stronger, sweeter, more pungent. Some specialists still grow Gros Michel bananas, and you can buy them . . . for a price!

M: There's an apocryphal story that artificial banana flavoring comes from those older bananas, and that's why banana candy never tastes like real bananas. That's likely untrue. There's a chemical in bananas that has that signature banana-y flavor, and it's cheap and easy to mass-produce, so candies use it. Gros Michel bananas have a lot more of this chemical, so even though they aren't the reason for banana candies, they do taste more like banana candy. A great example of the fact that correlation doesn't equal causation!

Humpback whales create a net of bubbles to catch fish.

Josie: A big group of whales will swim in circles, blow bubbles, and trap a school of fish. They then swoop in and gobble the fish up.

Olivia: That must require a ton of teamwork between the whales!

Josie: It does. But it gets even weirder: scientists think this is a *learned* behavior, not an instinctual one. Not every population of humpback whales knows how to bubble net feed.

Olivia: So they've just passed down the knowledge through the generations?

Josie: We're not sure, but that seems to be the case.

M: Humpback whales are one of the few success stories of endangered animals. Most of them came off the endangered animal list in 2016— their population has increased by eight times since the low point caused by whaling!

During a blood moon, you are seeing light from every sunrise and sunset on Earth at the exact same time.

Lloyd: If you were standing on the moon during a total lunar eclipse, and you looked at Earth, you would see a dark Earth with a fiery red ring around it. For half the world, that red ring is sunrise. For the other half of the world, that red ring is sunset. Every single sunrise and sunset that is occurring at that moment is reflected by the moon. And so to us standing here on Earth, the moon turns bloodred.

Olivia: It really is one of the coolest things to experience. I couldn't believe my eyes when I saw it for the first time.

Almost all gold in jewelry comes from meteorites.

Lloyd: So gold isn't actually rare on Earth—it's just that most of it is in the Earth's core! But we can't get to any of that gold. So almost all the gold that we mine on Earth actually comes from meteorites that hit Earth in our distant past. That ring on your finger right there is space gold!

Olivia: Ooooh, it feels more special now!

A wandering albatross has the longest wingspan of any bird and can spend up to six years at sea before returning to dry land.

Olivia: That's why there's that famous poem about the sailor who killed the albatross.

Dick: "The Rime of the Ancient Mariner" by Samuel Taylor Coleridge. It's why people say that something is an "albatross around their neck." In the poem, the sailor was cursed because he killed an albatross, and so his sailboat was trapped at sea without any wind.

M: It's also where the phrase "water, water everywhere and not a drop to drink" comes from, because the ship ran out of fresh water.

Clay tablets used in ancient Mesopotamia were reusable.

Dick: Clay is actually quite soft before you bake it, and most of the tablets they had were never baked. You'd write your message and send it over, then the next person would splash a little water on it to wipe it off and write something else.

Adam: Like an Etch A Sketch?

Dick: Exactly. Ironically, some of the best records we have from that era are libraries that were burned down, like the Library of Ashurbanipal. The Babylonian army wanted to erase it from history, but the fire actually *baked* the tablets and preserved them for us today.

M: Ironically, our very attempts to conceal information often preserve it. There's even a psychological phenomenon called the "Streisand effect," wherein attempts to suppress information leads to its spread—banned books are read more frequently, and censorship can backfire by making us talk more about a story.

But isn't that the beautiful thing about humans?

For thousands of years, we've had an unstoppable urge to share information with one another. Today, it might be fun facts. Yesterday, clay tablets. Before that, cave paintings.

When we first sat huddled around fires, in an icy world of mammoths and saber-toothed tigers and the endless unknown, our urge was not just to hunt and survive and procreate. Those things were important, sure—and without them you and I wouldn't be standing here today! But we did something more. We picked up some charcoal, we crushed up plants, and we drew something on the cave wall. Animals, maybe. Stories of the hunt. Handprints from children.

Why? Because, surrounded by the great unknown, we had the chance to make our small corner just a little bit more known.

We humans are hardwired to seek and share knowledge—sometimes a bit too much! I hope you enjoyed the party and we didn't overdo it— I know my friends can be a bit kooky, but I love them dearly. They do love trying to sound smart at parties, don't they?

But I think, in some ways, you were the smartest one here: because you really listened.

I'm glad to call you my friend, I really am. I do hope you'll attend my next party. I don't know when it will be or who will be attending (though I certainly hope these brilliant folks would be inclined to return). So keep an eye out for another invitation.

Until then, stay curious.

-M

Acknowledgments

Thank you to all the Idea Soup fans out there. If it weren't for you, none of this would exist. You give me faith in the world's ability to stay curious, continue asking questions, and get a little smarter every day. Especially at parties.

Above all, I'd like to thank my partner, Campbell, who tolerated countless sleepless nights as writing this book consumed my life for the last year and a half. Thank you for all your support, feedback, and for being in my life. I can't imagine writing this book without you.

Thank you to Colin Conwell, my best friend and intellectual partner who seemingly constitutes a partition of my brain. I often feel a thought has not been thunk clearly until I've discussed it with you. Your feedback on the structure and content of this book has been instrumental in its completion. You have talked me off many a ledge! The very theme of this book was inspired by the many real late night conversations we've had fueled by bad wine and good company. I'm forever grateful for our friendship.

Thank you to Chelsea Boccagno for providing such detailed feedback on so many different versions of this text. You have helped me develop my writing style over the years, always giving great feedback and pushing me to be a better writer since the days when I was writing blogs. Thank you also for your support of my mental health. You are a great friend and my life is better for having you in it.

Thank you to my editor, Alexander Rigby. Making this book was an incredibly complicated process but I feel like we've made something great together. Thanks for being so patient and supportive over the last year and a half. This book is as much yours as it is mine.

Thank you to Lindsay Dobbs for helping bring this book to life visually, especially designing such a great cover.

Thank you to Pat Corrigan for the amazing illustrations. Your illustrations are the blood and muscles around the bones of text in this book, and I appreciate you adding such great color to this story, especially bringing the characters to life.

Thank you to Mara Grunbaum for your exceptional fact-checking. Your academic rigor and thoroughness impressed the heck out of me and improved the quality of this book significantly. Truly some of the best research I've seen on these sorts of topics, which can be challenging to interrogate at times.

Thank you to Marko Todoroski for help with sourcing facts and assisting with Idea Soup research more broadly. I value our continued collaboration tremendously.

Thank you to my management team, Jared Ringel and Mike Sheffer. I'd be an unorganized mess without y'all. I love all the growth we've experienced and look forward to all that is to come.

Thank you to my family for the steadfast support over the years. I love you all and would not be the person I am today without you. Our dinner table was always full of stories, fun facts, and lively debates. There was a fire and a passion in the way we discussed history, science, politics, and art, and I hope that I never, ever forget that fire.

Thank you to Foster Daly and his team for visual consultation on the aesthetic of the book at a critical junction.

Thank you to Costa Ciminiello for listening to me complain when times got hard and always being a positive presence in my life.

Thank you to Jade for giving constant advice and support throughout the process, often dropping everything at the last minute to help. Your taste is impeccable and your feedback has been incredibly valuable.

Thank you to Zac Geoffray for a very thorough read-through of the book and the phenomenal advice on character development. You're brilliant in everything you do.

Thank you to Connor Franta for giving me detailed feedback in a time of extreme doubt, as well as support throughout the writing process. Hearing from a fellow writer made me feel a little less crazy and your perspective was incredibly valuable.

Thank you to DK Publishing for taking a chance on me and helping me accomplish my dream of becoming an author. I've always wanted to write a book, ever since I was a child. This is very, very special to me. When I was a kid, you published an "Eyewitness" history book that I read until the pages tore and the spine fell apart. You helped ignite my passion for history and science, and so it feels fitting that I've come full circle and can now add my small contribution to your library. I hope copies of this book become as ragged as those that I have loved.

Index

French Revolution, 154
Freud, Sigmund, 182
Freyja (Norse goddess), 172

G

Garfield, James, 102
Garfield the cat telephones, 84
Gasoline, 27, 92
gene therapy, 167
Genghis Khan, 147
geography
    Amazon River, 64
    country with the most islands, 96
    longest coastline, 153
Georgian language, 86
geosmin, 148
geothermal power, 34
Germany, 32, 90, 158
giant squids, 59
Gillette, King C., 91
global warming, Permian extinction and, 99
gods and goddesses, 22, 78, 172
gold, 192
Goodall, Jane, 134
"goodbye," leaving without saying, 158
GPS satellites, 120
Grant, Ulysses S., 117
Grateful Dead, 115
Gravity, 34, 120
greaser subculture, 82
Great Library of Alexandria, 76
Greece, ancient, 100, 107
Greek gods and goddesses, 22, 78
Green Day (band), 80
Greenland, sharks of, 116
Gros Michel bananas, 187
groundlings, in Shakespeare's audience, 145
guacamole, 18
guillotined heads, death masks of, 154
Guinness World Records, beginning of, 177

H

Habermas, Jürgen, 180
hadal zone, of the ocean, 60
Hákarl, 116
Hallucinogenics, 81, 114
Hanukkah, 160

Hawaii, leprosy in, 93
Hawing, Stephen, 160
Hawke, Bob, 19
health and disease. See also medicine
    eradication of malaria, 123
    miasma theory ("nigh air"), 122
    scaring Nazis away with a fictitious, 96
    scurvy, 130
    smallpox inoculations during the American
    Revolution, 140
    viruses causing the common cold, 118
Helios (Greek god), 22
helium, 22
Hemingway, Ernest, 80
hermaphrodites, 131
heroin, 113
hippie movement, CIA and, 115
hippos, 24
historical figures. See also Washington,
George
    Adolf Hitler, 91, 182
    Alexander the Great, 147
    Caligula (Roman emperor), 138
    Christopher Columbus, 71
    Genghis Khan, 147
    Julius Caesar, 163
    King Charles VIII of France, 42
    Martin Luther King, 151
    Paul Revere, 136
    Thomas Edison, 117, 143
    William Shakespeare, 145
history. See also ancient civilizations;
inventions; World War I; World War II
    British military theatrical companies during
    the American Revolution, 137
    Bronze Age Collapse, 100–101
    of coffee and coffeehouses, 180
    colonists on Roanoke Island, 135
    crop rotation, 46
    Great Library of Alexandria, 76
    Inca Empire, 68
    Mesopotamian tablets, 66
    Ottoman and Roman Empire, 163
    Pearl Harbor, 77
    Permian extinction, 99
    Prohibition, 112
    spreading of stories and facts in, 182
    sugar in, 89
Hitler, Adolf, 91, 182
holiday, Hanukkah, 160

Hollywood, California, 143
Holt, Harold, 19
hors d'Oeuvres, 13
horses, 83, 138
human body
    cell turnover in, 164
    growing faster during spring and summer, 149
    iron in, 141
    nail growth and, 75
    sensitive to smell of rain, 148
    vision of, 149
humpback whales, 188
hydrogen sulfide, 50

I

Ice Age, 15, 29
Iceland, 34, 116, 144
IKEA Effect, the, 56
"I'm not sure," saying, 174
Inca Empire, 68
indigenous populations, Christopher
  Columbus and, 71
Indus Valley Civilization, 103
interplanetary dust, false down and, 95
interrogator, Nazi, 152
Inuit people, scurvy and, 130
inventions
    Coca-Cola, 117
    disposable razor blades, 91
    heroin, 113
    of the iPhone, 16
    metal detector, 102
    moving sidewalks, 52
    penicillin, 51
    toilet paper, 35
    Velcro, 171
    of words and phrases by Shakespeare, 145
Irish exit/Irish goodbye, 158
iron, in the human body, 141
islands
    Alcatraz, 97
    country with the most, 96
    leper colony on Hawaiian, 93
    woolly mammoths on, 15
itchy noses, of Apollo astronauts, 17

J

Japan
    greaser/rockabilly subculture in, 82

how people wiped their butts in ancient, 107

length of a day shortened by earthquake in, 126

the Mongols and, 87

Pearl Harbor and, 77

pouring your own sake in, 32

Japanese language, 42

Jordan, Michael, 78

K

kamikazes, 87

kerosene, 50, 54

Kesey, Ken, 115

King, Martin Luther Jr., 151

knocker-uppers, 129

Kraken, the, 59

L

language(s) and linguistics. *See also* English language; words and word origins

Mayan, 183

Proto-Indo-European language, 42

translation of Mesopotamian tablets, 66

Latin America, 86

leaded gasoline, 27

leaders. *See also* politicians and political events

Caligula, 138

death of monarchs, 42

Genghis Khan, 147

Julius Caesar, 163

overthrowing Latin American dictators, 86

lead paint, 27, 28

lead sugar, 28

leafcutter ants, 43

leap seconds, 126

leeches, medical, 83

legislation

about pushing a moose out of an airplane, 119

on child labor, 89

on saying "sorry," 153

Leo XIII, Pope, 117

leprosy, 93

libraries

Great Library of Alexandria, 76

Library of Ashurbanipal, 196

light speed, gravity and, 34

Lloyd's Coffee House, 180

Loch Ness Monster, 59

London, England, sewer system, 35, 122

Lord Byron, 143

Los Angeles, Hollywood in, 143

Los Zetas (Mexican cartel), 86

Lovelace, Ada, 143

LSD, 114

M

main course meal, 63

malaria, 122, 123

manhole cover, 95

maps, for the Amazon River, 64

marketing ploys, 177

mathematics

average versus median statistics, 53

birthday paradox and, 70

number of ways to shuffle a deck, 23

The Matrix (film), 141

Mayans and Mayan language, 183

medicine

in the future, 167

leeches used in, 83

sugar and, 89

VIP syndrome, 102

megapixels, 149

Mercury, 55

Merry Pranksters, 115

MERS (camel-borne coronavirus), 118

Mesopotamia. *See* ancient Mesopotamia

meteorites, gold coming from, 192

Mexican cartel, 866

miasma theory, 122

Michelin star, origin of, 177

military. *See also* war(fare); World War I; World War II

facial hair and, 91

Nazi interrogator, 152

theatrical companies, 137

military school, "anti-communism," 86

MKUltra program, 114

monarchs, deaths of, 42

Mongols, the, 87, 147

mosaics, of Nazi interrogator, 152

mosquitoes, 24

Mount Everest, 178

Movies, 81, 141, 143

moving sidewalks, 52

music, 80, 115

muttonchops, 25

myth(s)

about Roman Emperor Caligula, 138

coming from fossil finds, 125

mythical creatures, 59

mythology, Norse, 172

N

nails. *See* fingernails

names

business, 78

changes in, 151

National Historic Park, 93

National Malaria Eradication Program, 123

Nazis, the, 95, 152

negative geotropism, 187

neutron star, weight of, 55

New Bedford, Massachusetts, 50

New Jersey, filing of movie patents in, 143

nicotine withdrawals, 20

Nike, 78

Nile River, 16

non-meat diet, 29

Noriega, Manuel Antonio, 86

Norse mythology, 172

Norway, 96

noses

astronauts scratching their, 17

breathing out of one nostril of, 67

"No Smoking" signs, 92

Notre-Dame cathedral, 164

nuclear reactors, 34

nuclear tests, 95

numeral system, base of 60, 175

O

ocean

Antarctic blue whale in, 60

deepest part of, 60

squids in the, 59

oil companies, leaded gasoline and, 27

Olympus Mons, 178

One Flew Over the Cuckoo's Nest (Kesey), 115

ostraca, 107

Ottoman Empire, 163

outer space and astronomy. *See also* solar system; sun, the

blood moon, 191

Sources

You can find the sources for all the facts listed in the book by scanning the QR code.

About the Author

Michael McBride is the educational content creator behind Idea Soup, a community of 1.5 million people who are curious about fun facts, bite-sized bits of history, and unique natural phenomena. Michael has traveled to 53 countries searching for interesting stories and speaks two languages poorly. He has a tendency to talk too much and feels very lucky anyone is listening at all.